PUPPET SCRIPTS BY THE MONTH

Margaret Cheasebro

BROADMAN PRESS
Nashville, Tennessee

© Copyright 1985 ● Broadman Press

4275-24

ISBN: 0-8054-7524-9

Dewey Decimal Classification: 791.5

Subject Heading: PUPPETS AND PUPPET PLAYS

Library of Congress Catalog Card Number: 84-20066

Printed in the United States of America

Library of Congress Cataloging in Publication Data

Cheasebro, Margaret, 1945-
    Puppet scripts by the month.

    1. Puppets and puppet-plays in Christian education.
I. Title.
BV1535.9.P8Cs   1985   246'.7   84-20066
ISBN 0-8054-7524-9 (pbk.)

Contents

December

January

I Resolve

Theme: Kindness
Scripture: Ephesians 4:31-32
Characters: Tom, Henry, Sheila

Tom: Eenie, meenie, minie, moe. Catch a tiger by the toe. If
         . . . .
Henry: What's up, Tom?
Tom: Hi, Henry. I'm trying to decide which new year's resolution
         I should list first.
Henry: How many do you have?
Tom: One hundred seventy-nine.
Henry: You're kidding!
Tom: Nope. My sister says I should have two hundred seventy-nine
         because I'm so rotten.
Henry: Why does she think you're rotten?
Tom: I don't know. Sisters are like that.
Henry: I'll bet she's still mad at you for taking her autograph book
         to show and tell.
Tom: Yeah. But the kids sure laughed at all that lovey-dovey stuff.
         I'll bet they'd really go wild if I took her diary to school.
Henry: You wouldn't do that, would you?
Tom: Probably not. But only because she keeps hiding it in a new
         place every night.
Henry: I'll bet I know what one of your resolutions is.
Tom: What?
Henry: Be nice to your sister.
Tom: Let's see. That's number 178.
Henry: Maybe that should be your first resolution.
Tom: Are you crazy? My first resolution is to chew twenty-five
         packs of gum a day and beat Andy Hubbard's record. Remember
         when he chewed twenty-four packs at school one day?
Henry: He didn't talk much the next day.
Tom: That's because he didn't work up to it. I'll practice for it every
         day like a marathon.
Henry (*discouraged*):   I've only got one resolution.
Tom: What is it?
Henry: To be nice to everyone.
Tom: That's the same one you had last year.
Henry: I know. I didn't do so well last year. I sort of flunked.
Tom: You're always nice to me.
Henry: That's because you're my best friend.
Tom: You're a smart kid to have me as your best friend.
Henry: Not really. You know the first time I broke my new year's
         resolution last year?

Tom: When?

Henry: Five minutes after I made it.

Tom: Oops.

Henry: I had "Be nice to everyone" written on a sheet of paper. I drew flowers and airplanes around it so I could hang it on my bedroom door. My mom saw it on the living room sofa when I went to get a drink. She thought it was junk and threw it out. I'd worked two hours on it. I got so mad I called her the garbage lady.

Tom: Uh oh.

Henry: I never made any more resolutions last year. I decided they were too hard to keep.

Tom: You sure are a nervy kid, calling your mother a garbage lady.

Henry: Not nervy enough to take my sister's autograph book to school.

Tom: Maybe I should be a little nicer to her. After all, she can't help it if she's a girl.

Henry: Why not make that your first resolution?

Tom: I don't know. I have so many resolutions, I can't remember them all.

Henry: Maybe one is enough.

Tom: Are you kidding? If I leave out the rest of the family, they'll be mad at me.

Henry: OK. Have a lot of resolutions. But let them each start, "I will be nice to. . . ." Then give a different name to each resolution.

Tom: OK. Let's see. Number one. I will be nice to my sister. Boy, that's tough. You know what she did yesterday? She ate all my chocolate bar, the whole thing. I had it in the fridge with a big sign that said, "Hands off, property of Tom."

Henry: Maybe you could resolve to be nice to your sister only when she's nice to you.

Tom: Yeah! That would be easy.

Henry: OK. Make that number one.

Tom: Wait a minute. That resolution's no different than I act now. Aren't resolutions supposed to help you act better?

Henry: Yeah. You'd better put down that you'll be nice to her all the time.

Tom: I guess so. For my next resolution I'll be nice to Mom and Dad all the time.

Henry: OK.

Tom: For number three I'll be nice to Spot.

Henry: You're resolving to be nice to your dog?

Tom: Why not? He has feelings too.

Henry: OK, OK, just asking.

Tom: I guess I'll throw out all these other resolutions.

Henry: Sure. Three's enough to keep you busy all year.

Tom: I'm really glad to get rid of number 127.

Henry: What was that?

Tom: To eat spinach every time Mom serves it.

Henry: Hmmm. Don't you think it would be breaking your resolu-
        tion to be nice to your mom if you didn't eat what she fixed for
        you?

Tom: Some friend you are! Well, maybe I'll take a taste of it just to
        please her.

Sheila (*from offstage*):   Tom!

Henry: That's your sister.

Tom: Not her again.

Henry: Remember your resolution.

Sheila (*enters*):   Tom, I've been looking all over for you. Hi, Henry.

Henry: Hi.

Tom: Oh, hi, Sheila.

Sheila: I just finished my new year's resolutions.

Tom: Me too.

Sheila:· You know what my first resolution is?

Tom: What?

Sheila: Not to get mad at you.

Tom: That's a good resolution.

Henry: Tell her yours.

Sheila: Yeah, tell me yours.

Tom: It's . . . it's a secret.

Sheila: Ah, Tommy, you're embarrassed. I'll bet you resolved not to
        keep trying to find my diary.

Tom: How did you know I've been looking for your diary?

Sheila: Big sisters know everything.

Tom: No, they don't.

Sheila: They do too.

Tom: OK, if you know so much, what's my resolution?

Sheila: Give me a minute, and I'll tell you.

Tom: See, you don't know.

Henry: Psst, Tom, don't break your resolution already.

Tom: I'm trying to be nice to her, but she's so. . . .

Sheila (*interrupts*): Aha, I know! You resolved to be nice to me.

Tom: No fair. Henry made me tell.

Sheila: Henry's a good kid. And so are you—for a kid brother. If I can keep my resolution and you can keep yours, we'll get along great this year.

Tom: I guess that's one way of being nice to our parents when we're nice to each other.

Sheila: You're such a good kid I'll give you a kiss.

Tom: Yuck! (*Tries to move away as Sheila kisses him.*)

Henry: This is all so touching, I think I'll go home.

Tom: You're lucky not to have a kissy-kissy sister.

Henry: Your sister's not so bad.

Sheila: You're all right, Henry. I'll mention you in my diary tonight.

Henry: Bye. (*Exits.*)

Tom: Just because of my resolution, don't think your diary is safe from me.

Sheila: I'd never make that mistake, and I'm not going to get mad at you either.

Tom: Hey, you didn't get mad. You're usually shouting by this time.

Sheila: I'm doing pretty well, aren't I? Let's go tell Mom and Dad about our resolutions before we slip up and break them.

(*Tom and Sheila exit.*)

January

New Year's Resolutions

Theme: Putting Up with Others' Faults
Scripture: Colossians 3:12-13
Characters: Martha, Ferdinand, Bernie, Atlas

Martha: Happy new year to me,
        Happy new year to me,
        Happy new year, dear Martha,
        Happy new year. . . .

Ferdinand (*appears*): What are you doing, Martha?

Martha: I'm singing happy new year to me.

Ferdinand: You mean to myself.

Martha: Not to you. To me.

Ferdinand: Oh, forget it. I don't know why I try to improve your grammar, anyway. It never works.

Martha: That's what's wrong with you, Ferdinand. You're always so negative.

Ferdinand: I am not.

Martha: You are too.

Ferdinand: Am not.

Martha: See? All those nots and nevers. You say them all the time.

Ferdinand: Only when I'm around you.

Martha: We'll see about that. (*Hollers.*) Bernie! Get up here.

Bernie (*grumpily from offstage*): You don't have to shout. (*Enters.*) I can hear. What do you want?

Martha: Ferdinand here claims he's only negative around me. I think he's negative almost all the time. We want you to decide who's right.

Bernie: I can't believe this. You called me all the way up here to decide a dumb thing like that?

Ferdinand: Yeah, dumb. That's what I call it too.

Martha: Well, if I'd known you were going to be so temperamental, I would of went to Atlas for help.

Ferdinand: I would have gone.

Martha: Well, why didn't you?

Ferdinand: No, no. I mean you should say I would have gone instead of I would of went.

Martha: Would you quit bugging me about the way I talk? You see what I mean, Bernie? He's always so negative.

Bernie: I think you both stink, and the next time you call me up here for something so dumb, I'm going to punch you both in the nose.

Atlas (*appears between Bernie and Martha*): Looks like I got here just in time. You three are always fighting. I never saw the like.

Bernie: Thank goodness you're here, Atlas. I was taking a nice nap when Mopmouth Martha here calls me.

Martha: Watch who you call a mopmouth. If I'd have known you you were asleep, I would of saw to it that a whole band played "Rise and Shine" outside your window.

Ferdinand: Not would of saw. It's would have seen.

Martha: Oh, shut up, you goon.

Ferdinand: Watch who you call a goon, you dimwit.

Atlas: All right, cut it out. You'd think you were all two-year-olds. You ought to be ashamed of yourselves. (*Thinks.*) I have an idea. It's obvious we all need to make some improvements. So why don't we each make one new year's resolution and try to keep it for the rest of the day?

Bernie: That's a great idea. I know what mine will be.

Atlas: What?

Bernie: To punch Martha in the nose the first chance I get.

Atlas: Now, Bernie. That's no way to be. You've got to think of something that will make you a better person.

Ferdinand: Fat chance. It will never work.

Martha: See? He's negative even around you guys. I knowed I was right.

Ferdinand: Knew, Martha, not knowed.

Atlas (*to audience*):   Oh, dear. Oh, dear. This is going to take some careful handling. (*To Bernie, Martha, and Ferdinand.*) I'll tell you what. How about if I make a suggestion for each one of you. If you like it, that can be your resolution. If not, you can think up another one for yourself.

Martha, Bernie, and Ferdinand: OK.

Atlas: Ferdinand, how about if you resolve to be more positive?

Ferdinand: Positive?

Atlas: Yes. Don't say things can't be done or tear other people down when they do something wrong.

Ferdinand: You think I'm negative too?

Atlas: Sometimes. If you try a little positiveness now and then, I think you'll be happier and have more friends.

Ferdinand: Just for the rest of the day?

Atlas: You only have to do it today.

Ferdinand: OK, but if I decide I don't like it, I won't do it tomorrow.

Atlas: That's good enough for me. Now, Martha, why don't you try improving your grammar?

Martha: I don't need no improvement.

Ferdinand: Any improvement, not no. . . .

Atlas (*interrupts*):   No fair, Ferdinand. You can't break your new year's resolution until tomorrow.

Martha: I guess I can work on my grammar, but only for today!

Atlas: Good for you. Now, Bernie, you need to try controlling your temper better.

Bernie: There's nothing wrong with my temper!

Atlas: You're right. Your bad temper is very healthy and gets lots of exercise. What you need to do is exercise your good temper more. No more threats to punch people in the nose.

Bernie: OK, but only until the day is over.

Ferdinand: Now that we all have a resolution, what about you, Atlas?

Atlas: Oh, dear, I forgot all about myself.

Ferdinand: You did such a good job giving us resolutions that maybe you should give yourself one too.

Atlas: I wish I could, but my mind is blank. I've been so busy helping you guys, I haven't done anything about myself.

Martha: Maybe that would be a good resolution for you.

Atlas: What would?

Martha: To spend more time taking care of the things you need to do for yourself.

Ferdinand: Hey, yeah.

Bernie: I think you've done it, Martha.

Martha: I have?

Atlas: I think you're right. That would be a good resolution for me. Here's another resolution for all of us. It may be the hardest of all to keep.

Ferdinand: Oh, no. The ones you gave us are hard enough.

Martha: Don't be negative.

Bernie: Oh, leave him alone, Martha. What's the other one, Atlas? We won't promise to keep it, but at least we can hear it.

Atlas: It comes from the Bible. Proverbs 3:5-6 says, "Trust in the Lord with all thine heart; and lean not unto thine own understanding. In all thy ways acknowledge him, and he shall direct thy paths."

Bernie: Whew! That's a lot for one resolution.

Martha: It sure is.

Ferdinand: I don't know if we can do all that.

Atlas: Maybe you're right. How about if we divide it up?

Martha: How do you do that?

Atlas: Like this. Martha, your part will be, "Trust in the Lord with all thine heart." Bernie, yours will be, "And lean not unto thine own understanding." Ferdinand, you'll have, "In all thy ways acknowledge him." And mine will be, "And he shall direct thy paths."

Bernie: OK. That makes it easier.

Atlas: Now, let's try to say our parts and see how they sound. Martha, you start.

Martha: Trust in the Lord with all thine heart.

Atlas: Now you, Bernie.

Bernie: And lean not unto thine own understanding.

Atlas: Ferdinand.

Ferdinand: In all thy ways acknowledge him.

Atlas: And he shall direct thy paths.

Bernie: We sound like a choir.

Ferdinand: Let's say it again. Maybe those people out there will say it with us.

Atlas: OK.

Martha: Trust in the Lord with all thine heart.

Bernie: And lean not unto thine own understanding.

Ferdinand: In all thy ways acknowledge him.

Atlas: And he shall direct thy paths.

Ferdinand: All right! I think if we can remember that, we can keep our new year's resolutions better.

Bernie: Yeah. But we'll have to stick together so we'll have all the parts in the verses.

Martha: If we say it long enough, we'll know everybody else's part.

Atlas: Let's go share our resolutions with the neighbors across the street.

(*All exit.*)

February

Me? Love a Bully?

Theme: Love Your Enemies
Scripture: Proverbs 25:21-22
Characters: Linda, Buster, Hank, Mom

Linda: You sure are walking fast. Are you that excited about going home from school?

Buster: I'm so mad I could hit somebody.

Linda: What's wrong?

Buster: It's that bully, Hank. You remember that math homework paper I worked on so hard last night?

Linda: The one with all the multiplication tables?

Buster: Yeah. On the way to school today, he grabbed my math book and threw it on the ground. My homework paper fell out, and the wind blew it away.

Linda: Why did he grab your book?

Buster: He said he felt mean this morning, and I was the closest person to him.

Linda: That's terrible.

Buster: When my teacher asked where my homework was and I told her the wind blew it away, she didn't believe me.

Linda: Why didn't you tell her about Hank?

Buster: He was sitting in the second row glaring at me the whole time. If I had told on him, I'd have gotten a knuckle sandwich at lunch time.

Linda: I'm glad he's not in my grade.

Buster: If I don't want to get an F, I have to do that homework over again tonight.

Linda: I don't have any homework. I can help you.

Buster: How? You aren't into multiplication yet.

Linda: Maybe I could make you some hot chocolate while you do your homework.

Buster: With marshmallows in it?

Linda: Yeah.

Buster: Oh, boy! I'll race you home. (*Runs.*)

Linda: No fair. You got a headstart.

Buster: I touched the stairs first. I win!

Linda: You cheated.

Buster: What are you griping about? You don't have to do your math paper over again.

Linda: Oh, shut up. Hi, Mom, we're home.

Mom (*appears*):   Hi, kids. How was school?

Buster: Terrible.

Mom: How come?

Buster: That bully Hank threw my math book down. My homework paper fell out and blew away, and I have to do it over tonight or I'll get an F. I hate that bully.

Linda: Yeah. We hate him.

Mom: What good does it do to hate him?

Buster: It makes me feel better.

Linda: Me too.

Mom: When I was in school, there was a bully in my class too.

Buster: There was?

Mom: One day after Christmas I wore a ribbon in my hair that my grandmother gave me for Christmas. It was a big, velvety blue ribbon, the prettiest thing I'd ever seen. In school the bully who sat behind me took his scissors and cut it all up.

Linda: Oh, no!

Mom: When I got home that night, I cried and cried. You know what my mother told me?

Buster: What?

Mom: To go back to school the next day and tell that bully I forgave him and that with Jesus' help I would love him.

Buster: I thought Grandma was smart until just now.

Linda: I'd never forgive him. I'd punch him out.

Buster: You're too little.

Linda: I am not.

Buster: You are too.

Mom: People are almost always small enough to fight. They're not always big enough to love. Both of you are big enough to love a bully.

Linda: We are?

Buster: Were you big enough to love that bully, Mom?

Mom: I didn't think so, but my mother did. She sat me down and read to me out of 1 Corinthians 13, where it says that love is not easily provoked and keeps no record of wrongs.

Buster: I know what that means. It means love doesn't hold grudges.

Mom: That's right. And when you're mad at that bully, you're holding a grudge.

Buster: But, Mom, it's too hard to love him. On the other hand, if I punch Hank, he'll hit me back, and I'll get in trouble for starting a fight. I guess I'll just redo my homework and try to ignore Hank.

Mom: That's the easy way out.

Buster: It's not easy doing my homework over again.

Linda: Yeah, and it's not easy making him hot chocolate while he does his homework.

Mom: It's easier than loving Hank.

Buster: How could anyone love Hank?

Mom: Maybe that's his problem.

Buster: What's his problem?

Linda: Yeah, what's his problem?

Mom: Maybe nobody loves Hank.

Buster: I believe it. He's so mean nobody would want to love him.

Mom: That's just it. Maybe he's mean because nobody loves him.

Linda: You mean if Buster loved him, he'd stop being mean?

Mom: Maybe.

Buster: But, Mom! I can't love that creep.

Mom: That's what I thought about my bully. But then I asked Jesus to help me love him, and it wasn't so hard any more.

Buster: Did you tell him you loved him?

Mom: No. I just took him a big juicy red apple to school the next day and told him Jesus loved him and I would try to be his friend.

Buster: What did he say?

Mom: That's the funny part. He didn't say anything. He just got a funny look on his face. He took the apple, put it in his pocket, and walked away.

Linda: He didn't even say thank you?

Mom: No.

Buster: Isn't that just like a bully!

Mom: The next day at school he brought me a box. You know what was in it?

Buster: A spider.

Linda: Or a grasshopper.

Mom: There was a blue velvet ribbon in it, not as pretty as the one Grandma gave me, but it was still pretty. He sort of shoved it in my hand and said he was sorry he cut up my ribbon. Then he gulped and said nobody ever said they would try to be his friend before.

Buster: That's a neat story, Mom. But Hank has a friend. He's bigger than Hank is, and they walk around the playground at recess threatening people.

Linda: Hank probably wouldn't have cut up your ribbon, Mom. He would have *eaten* it.

Mom: Maybe he has that older friend because nobody his age will be his friend.

Buster: Yeah. He's so mean nobody wants to go near him.

Mom: Well, kids. I've got to see a friend. I'll be back in an hour. But before I go, here's the ingredients for the hot chocolate, Linda. Do you remember how we made it last week?

Linda: Yeah.

Mom: Be good. Bye. (*She exits.*)

Linda: I'll make your hot chocolate now.

Buster: OK. Put in lots of chocolate.

Linda: This is fun. It's the first time I ever made hot chocolate by myself. Hey, Buster, I've got an idea.

Buster: What?

Linda: Why don't you call Hank on the phone. Tell him you'll try to be his friend and invite him over for some hot chocolate.

Buster: Are you crazy? He'd probably swear at me.

Linda: Maybe not.

Buster: If you were me, would you call him?

Linda: Sure.

Buster: Baloney. You'd probably hide in your room.

Linda: Give a brother a good idea and look what you get. Abuse.

Buster: It was a lousy idea.

Linda: Maybe. But I'll bet if you wait till tomorrow to tell him you'll try to be his friend, you'll never tell him.

Buster: Who says I'm going to tell him that at all?

Mom: That's what Mom told her bully.

Buster: Her bully was different.

Linda: Big deal! While I make this hot chocolate, you know what I'm doing?

Buster: What?

Linda: Asking God to fill it so full of love that when Hank drinks it, he'll know you really do want to be his friend.

Buster: You're weird. I don't even know if I want to be his friend.

Linda: Wouldn't Mom be surprised if she came home to find Hank here?

Buster: Would you cut that out? I'm going to my bedroom to do my homework. (*Exits.*)

Linda: God, please fill this hot chocolate full of love.

Buster (*enters*):   I can't concentrate on my math.

Linda: How come?

Buster: I keep thinking about your dumb idea of calling Hank. I guess I'll just call him.

Linda: Good. Just to be safe, I'll put a little more chocolate in this hot chocolate. And some salt and some pancake syrup. That should make it extra good. What's this? Curry powder? Must be good or Mom wouldn't have it. I'll put some in.

Buster: Where's the phone book?

Linda: I don't know.

Buster: I found it under the sofa cushion. Let's see. Brandon. That's in the Bs. Here it is. The only Brandon in the book. I knew he was one of a kind. OK, Linda, if this doesn't work, it's your fault.

Linda: God, you heard him. Keep the love pouring into this hot chocolate.

Buster: Hello. Is Hank there? This is Hank? Uh, hi, this is Buster. You know, the Buster in school. The one whose math book you threw on the ground today. Well, I wanted to say—uh—I forgive you. And to say that—uh—Jesus loves you, and I'll try to be your friend.

Linda: Don't forget about the hot chocolate.

Buster: How about coming over to my house for some hot chocolate? No, it's not a trick. I just want to show you I really want to be your friend. OK, I promise to take the first drink out of your cup. Come over right now. I live across the street from the convenience store on Elm Street in a big yellow house. OK. Bye.

Buster: He's coming. But he thinks we're trying to poison him.

Linda: We'll show him. This hot chocolate will be so full of love it will convince him.

Buster: Maybe I'd better have some of that hot chocolate now. I don't feel full of love at all. I'd like to punch that jerk right in the nose.

Linda: Someone's knocking on the door.

Buster: Oh-oh. What if that's him?

Linda: Better answer it.

Buster: Hi, Hank. Come in.

Hank (*enters*): You guys don't fool me. I know this is some kind of trick.

Buster: It's no trick. Honest. I really want to be your friend.

Hank: Who do you think you're kidding?

Buster: I'm still kind of sore at you, Hank, because I still have to do that math paper over. But Jesus told us to love each other and not hold grudges. I'm a Christian, and I want to do the things Jesus told us to do.

Hank: You're really something. Anybody here besides you?

Buster: Just my little sister. She's making hot chocolate.

Hank: Just your sister?

Buster: Yeah.

Hank: That's all?

Buster: Yeah.

Hank: Maybe you really are on the level.

Buster: What's the matter? Did you think I'd have the whole class over here to beat you up?

Hank: Something like that.

Buster: I really do want to be your friend.

Linda: Come get some hot chocolate.

Buster: OK. Still want me to take the first taste from your cup?

Hank: Yeah.

Linda: Here, Hank, a nice big cup for you.

Hank: After you, Buster.

Linda: We're not trying to poison you, Hank. We love you.

Buster (*sips*):   Yikh! This is terrible, Linda. What did you do to make it taste so bad?

Linda: It can't be bad. It's got love in it.

Hank (*skeptically*):   Sure it does. I'm leaving.

Linda: Wait. You can't leave before you taste this. Here, I'll taste it too if you'll taste it.

Hank: Well, nothing happened to Buster. OK. But you go first.

Linda: (sips) Ooh. You're right, Buster. It isn't very good.

Hank: Here, let me taste. (*Sips.*) Reminds me a little of pancakes and syrup—and something else. It's not so bad.

Buster: You mean you like it?

Hank: No, but I don't think you were trying to poison me. I guess you two are all right.

Mom (*enters*):   Well, who have we here?

Buster: Hi, Mom. This is our friend, Hank.

Hank: They made me some hot chocolate.

Mom: That sounds good. Pour me a cup.

Linda: I don't think you'll like it. I put too much something in it.

Mom (*sips*):   Ooh! You're right, dear. Why don't I make another batch?

Buster: All right! My mom is a great hot chocolate maker.

Hank: While she makes the hot chocolate, why don't we do your math homework, Buster?

Buster: You mean it?

Hank: Sure. After all, what are friends for? (*Hank and Buster exit.*)

Linda: My hot chocolate wasn't very good, Mom. But God put a lot of love in it.

Mom: He sure did. But he didn't put it in the hot chocolate. He put it inside you and Buster. That's the love that Hank responded to. Now let's take this new batch of hot chocolate to the boys.

(*Linda and Mom exit.*)

February

The Valentine's Day Gift

Theme: Friendship
Scripture: Proverbs 17:17
Characters: Henry, Myrtle

Henry (*pacing feverishly up and down*): What am I going to do?
     Tomorrow is Valentine's Day, and I don't have a valentine for
     my best friend.

Myrtle (*enters*): Why are you pacing all over the place, Henry?

Henry: Oh, Myrtle, I'm so upset. It's almost Valentine's Day, and I
     don't have a valentine for my best friend.

Myrtle: Why don't you go to the store and get her a box of candy?

Henry: That's too easy. I want to give her something special, some-
     thing nobody else would give her.

Myrtle: Maybe you could give her a broom.

Henry: A broom!?

Myrtle: Well, nobody else would give her one.

Henry: Stop being silly. Anyway, she's not a very good housekeep-
     er. Her room is always messy.

Myrtle: So is mine. Maybe you could get her a ring or a necklace.

Henry: She doesn't like jewelry.

Myrtle: Neither do I. Let's see, you could make her a Valentine's
     Day card.

Henry: I'm not very good at things like that. It would take me
     forever to make one.

Myrtle: Oh.

Henry: Figuring out a good valentine is awfully hard. If I knew who
     started this valentine custom, I'd give him a piece of my mind.

Myrtle: Just because it's a custom, you don't have to do it.

Henry: I know, but it's fun.

Myrtle: You don't sound like you're having fun to me.

Henry: Once I think of a good valentine, then I'll have fun giving
     it. But right now, I'm so worried. I want this to be a special
     Valentine's Day for my friend. But without a gift it will be awful.

Myrtle: Cheer up. You'll think of something. If I were you, I'd give
     your best friend a big smile and spend some time with her on
     Valentine's Day.

Henry: But I'm supposed to *give* her something.

Myrtle: You'd be giving her your time. If you don't think that's
     enough, then do something for her.

Henry: Like what?

Myrtle: How should I know? I think all this valentine stuff is kind
     of dumb. Show her how fast you can run around the block. Bring
     her something good to eat like a pecan pie.

Henry: She already knows how fast I can run, and she makes delicious pecan pies. Her mom showed her how, and now she makes better pecan pies than anybody.

Myrtle: I'm pretty good at making pecan pies myself.

Henry: And I love to eat them.

Myrtle: I know you'll think of something to give your friend. (*Exits.*)

Henry: Oh, dear, oh, dear. What am I going to do? Myrtle doesn't know it, but she's my best friend, and she doesn't even care about valentines. What am I going to do for her? What does she need? Hey, maybe that's what I could do for her. I could help her clean her room. (*Exits.*)

(*Henry reenters.*)

Henry: What a good night's sleep I had! I'm all rested for the big task of cleaning up Myrtle's room for Valentine's Day. (*Walks across the stage.*) Knock, knock. Myrtle, it's Henry. Let me in.

Myrtle: What are you doing here?

Henry: Happy Valentine's Day. I came to clean up your room.

Myrtle: Why?

Henry: Because it's Valentine's Day and you're my best friend, and your room is dirty.

Myrtle: I guess you're right. It could use a little cleaning. Come on in.

Henry: You can say that again. Yours is the only room I know that looks like a wastebasket.

Myrtle: What a rotten thing to say!

Henry: Well, it's true. Hey, what's that delicious smell?

Myrtle: It's nothing.

Henry: It smells like pecan pie.

Myrtle: You're right. It's a pecan pie for you. Happy Valentine's Day.

Henry: For me?

Myrtle: Yeah. Because it's Valentine's Day, and you're my best friend.

Henry: Wow! That's my favorite pie.

Myrtle: Come on, let's have a piece. Then you can help me clean up my room.

Henry: You're on! I love Valentine's Days!

(*Both exit.*)

March

Waiting for Spring with a Gappy Grin

Theme: Facing Problems
Scripture: 1 Corinthians 10:13
Characters: Lucy, Tom

Lucy: Ouch!

Tom: What's wrong?

Lucy: My tooth hurts.

Tom: Have you got a cavity?

Lucy: No, a loose tooth. Every time I touch it, it hurts.

Tom: I'll fix that. Let me see that tooth.

Lucy: Oh, no you don't. The last time I showed you a loose tooth, you tried to yank it out.

Tom: I remember. You bit my finger. I still have a scar.

Lucy: Serves you right.

Tom: If you won't let me pull your loose tooth, you could go to a dentist and have him take it out.

Lucy: I hate going to dentists. Anyway, when this tooth is ready to come out, it will.

Tom: You females are just alike!

Lucy: I know. We're all smart.

Tom: Ha! When I asked Mom why spring doesn't hurry up and get here, she said when it's ready to come, it will. That's all you females ever say—when it's ready to come, it will.

Lucy: That's because it's true. God made spring and teeth that way. I just wish teeth wouldn't take so long getting ready to fall out. I'm getting tired of loose teeth, and I'm tired of winter.

Tom: Me too. I want the leaves to turn green and flowers to grow and baseball season to get here. And I can hardly wait for your tooth to fall out.

Lucy (*woefully*):   When it does, I'll have a big hole right in the middle of my smile.

Tom: You'll be like Alice next door.

Lucy: She can't talk right without her front teeth. I'll probably sound like her and go around saying thpagetti, thpring, and thomerthault.

Tom: And dentitht.

Lucy: Oh, hush. (*Worried.*) I don't think I want my tooth to come out.

Tom: If it doesn't, the new permanent one won't grow in.

Lucy: But I'll look and sound so ugly.

Tom: Yeah, just like the trees in winter without their leaves.

Lucy: They look all dead, like sticks.

Tom: When you lose that tooth, I'll call you Miss Hole in the Head.

Lucy: You nerd! If you call me that, I'll steal your baseball glove. Then you'll be sorry!

Tom: You wouldn't! Just for that, I ought to pry open your mouth and yank out that tooth right now.

Lucy: You wouldn't dare! Wait till you get another loose tooth. I'll tie a string around it when you're snoring with your mouth open. Then I'll yank out *your* tooth.

Tom: I'd wake up before you got two feet from my bed. You don't scare me.

Lucy: Hmph! Remember how your last tooth came out?

Tom: Yeah. I was playing tag with the kids next door and ran into a tree. Clunk. Out came my tooth.

Lucy: You had a big hole right in the middle of your mouth.

Tom: Yeah. I made some kids at school pay twenty-five cents to see the tooth that came out of that hole. I got over two dollars in one day. It was great.

Lucy: You could do that. I couldn't. It's OK for boys to have gappy smiles, but girls are supposed to look pretty all the time.

Tom: Says who?

Lucy: I don't know. That's just the way it is.

Tom: There you go with that female phrase—just the way it is. You're wacko!

Lucy: Prove it.

Tom: OK. Think about the trees with all their leaves gone.

Lucy: What about them?

Tom: They all look like sticks in winter without leaves, whether they're male or female.

Lucy: How dumb you are! Trees aren't like people.

Tom: That's true. Instead of losing their teeth once in a long while like humans do, trees lose their leaves every fall. Then every spring they get them back. When kids outgrow their baby teeth, they get bigger ones. That's the way God planned it. So if boys can have gappy grins, girls can look that way too.

Lucy: Yeah? Well, if I can have a gappy grin, when I show kids the tooth that came out of my hole, I'm going to charge them fifty cents!

Tom: Nobody's going to pay fifty cents to look at a dumb tooth.

Lucy: They might. If ten people looked at it, I would have five dollars. Wow! Maybe losing teeth isn't so bad. But I'm glad people don't lose their teeth every year. Then we'd look and sound strange most of the time.

Tom: You're strange all the time.

Lucy: Cut that out!

Tom: I want to *yank* it out. That loose tooth would stop hurting you if you'd just open your mouth and let me pull it.

Lucy: Oh, no. We don't pull leaves off trees. They just fall off when they're ready. That's what this tooth is going to do too.

Tom: Oh, all right. Hey, how about playing doctor?

Lucy: OK.

Tom: I'll be the doctor. Open your mouth and say ahhh so I can see your throat.

Lucy: Wait a minute! You don't fool me. You just want to grab my tooth. I'll sure be glad when baseball season gets here. Then you won't be around so much to bug me.

Tom: Just for that, I'll chase you all over to make up for the time I won't be here to tease you.

Lucy: You'll never catch me. (*Runs offstage.*)

Tom: We'll see about that! (*Exits.*)

Lucy (*from offstage*):   Ouch!

Tom (*from offstage*):   What happened?

Lucy (*enters*):   I fell into the sofa and knocked out my tooth.

Tom: Let's see.

Lucy: Hand over the fifty cents first.

Tom: You wouldn't charge your own brother, would you?

Lucy: Yep.

Tom: Why, you traitor.

Lucy: You gave me the idea.

Tom: Oh, all right.

Lucy: Whoopee! Losing teeth isn't half bad.

(*Both exit.*)

March

Aren't Finders Keepers?

Theme: Honesty
Scripture: Leviticus 19:11
Characters: Mandy, Jane, Jane's Mother, Angela

Note: Should Easter fall in March instead of April, this script may be used in April, and April's Easter script, "Forgiving is an Easter Thing to Do," used in March.

Jane: Look what I found, Mandy.

Mandy: What?

Jane: A red leather wallet. It has a dog's head design on it, and it's got money inside.

Mandy: How much?

Jane: Eighteen dollars.

Mandy: Wow! Where did you find it?

Jane: On the school playground by the swings.

Mandy: I wonder whose it is.

Jane: I don't know. There's no name inside. Just a picture of an old lady.

Mandy: What are you going to do?

Jane: Maybe I should turn it in to lost and found.

Mandy: I guess you should.

Jane: But since there's no name inside, maybe I could keep it. I saw a pair of shorts in the store yesterday for $10.95. I sure liked them. But I couldn't ask Mom and Dad to buy them because they hardly have enough money for groceries.

Mandy: It sounds like you could use the money.

Jane: Do you think it would be wrong to keep the wallet?

Mandy: I don't know. Like you said, since there's no name in it . . . . Besides, aren't finders keepers?

Jane: Yeah, I guess so.

Mandy: I've got to go. See you later.

(*Both exit, then reenter.*)

Mandy: Wow, what a neat pair of shorts. I love those red, white, and blue stripes.

Jane: Me too. It's the prettiest pair of shorts I ever had.

Mandy: How did you ever talk your parents into buying them?

Jane: I didn't. I bought them myself.

Mandy: You?! Oh, I know. You spent the money you found in that wallet yesterday.

Jane: Yeah. It felt good to walk into the store all by myself and buy my own clothes.

Mandy: I wish I'd found the wallet.

Jane: It's like a birthday present.

Mandy: Look who's coming.

(*Angela enters.*)

Jane: Hi, Angela.

Angela (*sadly*):   Hi.

Mandy: What's wrong?

Angela: I've just ruined my grandmother's birthday.

Jane: How?

Angela: I saved up my money all year to buy her an electric can
    opener. She wants one but can't afford it. With last week's allow-
    ance, I had enough money. Then I lost my wallet.

Jane: Uh . . . you did?

Mandy: That's too bad.

Angela: I lost it yesterday. I was swinging on the school playground.
    Then I went home, and it was gone.

Jane: I'm sorry.

Angela: If you find it, will you let me know?

Mandy: Sure. What does it look like?

Angela: It's a red leather wallet with a picture of a dog's head on
    it. My grandma's picture is inside it and eighteen dollars. I sure
    hope I find it soon. Grandma's birthday is tomorrow.

Mandy: A red wallet with a dog's head?

Angela: Yeah.

Jane: We haven't seen it, but if we find it, we'll let you know.

Angela: Thanks. (*Exits.*)

Mandy: Jane, that sounds like the wallet you found.

Jane (*sadly*):   I know.

Mandy: What are you going to do?

Jane (*defensively*):   Why should I do anything? She lost it. And she
    was dumb enough not to put her name in it so people would
    know whose it was. Besides, you said finders are keepers.

Mandy: I guess I did. I really like your shorts. See you later.
    (*Exits.*)

Jane (*mimicking Mandy*):   What are you going to do? It's none of
    her business. I found that wallet fair and square. (*Exits.*)

(*Mother and Jane enter.*)

Mother: Jane, what a lovely pair of shorts. Where did you get them?

Jane: Hi, Mom. Mandy gave them to me.

Mother: That was awfully nice of her. They fit just right.

Jane: Yeah.

Mother: Don't you like them? You don't sound very enthusiastic.

Jane: They're fine. I guess I just don't feel very well.

Mother: Have a chocolate chip cookie. Maybe that will perk you up.

Jane: No, thanks.

Mother: If you're turning down your favorite cookie, you *must* not be feeling well.

Jane: I'm OK. Just, uh, I have, it's a stomachache, that's all.

Mother: Go lie down. Maybe it will go away.

Jane: OK. (*Exits.*)

(*Knock is heard on door.*)

Mother: Hello, Mandy.

Mandy: Hi. Is Jane here?

Mother: Yes. She's lying down. She has a stomachache.

Mandy: Oh.

Mother: Thanks for the lovely pair of shorts you gave Jane.

Mandy: I didn't give Jane. . . . I mean, oh yeah, sure. You're welcome. I didn't need them.

Mother: Hmmm. I have a feeling there's more to this than you're telling me.

Mandy: Uh . . . Hey, that's a good joke, Mrs. Martin. There's more to me than there should be. That's why I gave the shorts to Jane.

Mother: But, Mandy, you're smaller than Jane, and the shorts fit her fine.

Mandy: Oh. Well, looks are deceiving.

Mother: Something strange is going on. (*Calls out.*) Jane, come here.

Jane (*enters*): Yeah, Mom? Oh, hi, Mandy.

Mother: Something isn't right, and both of you know what it is. But you're both big enough to decide what to do. So I'm not going to ask you where you got those shorts, Jane. But if you didn't get them fair and square, I hope you'll do whatever is necessary to make things right.

Jane (*sniffles*): Oh, Mother. I did a terrible thing. I found a wallet and spent the money in it for these shorts.

Mandy: There was no name in the wallet. She didn't know whose it was so she could return it.

Jane: I went to the store and got these shorts. Then Angela told us she lost her wallet. It was the one I found. But I'd already spent the money.

Mother: How much money was in it?

Jane: Eighteen dollars.

Mother: That's a lot. What do you think you ought to do?

Jane (*meekly*): Pay her back.

Mother: Where will you get the money?

Jane (*sobs*): I don't know.

Mandy: Maybe you could take back the shorts.

Jane: I already got them dirty.

Mother: What about the money in your piggy bank?

Jane: My allowance money? But, Mother, it took me a long time to save ten dollars. I'm trying to buy a pair of roller skates.

Mother: Girls, you have a problem. But you're going to have to work it out yourselves. (*Exits.*)

Jane: What am I going to do?

Mandy: Maybe we could secretly borrow the money from my mother's purse.

Jane: That would be stealing. I've already spent somebody else's money, then lied to Angela and Mom. I feel awful. What am I going to do?

Mandy: How much money do you have left from the eighteen dollars?

Jane: Six dollars and fifty-five cents.

Mandy: With the ten dollars from your allowance, you'd have sixteen dollars and fifty-five cents.

Jane: That's not enough.

Mandy: I have a dollar and fifty cents I could lend you.

Jane: You do?

Mandy: Yeah.

Jane: You're really swell, Mandy. But how are we going to get the money to Angela?

Mandy: Maybe your mom could drive us. I know where Angela lives.

Jane: But I don't want her to know I spent her money. Maybe we could just slip the wallet into her mailbox.

Mandy: Someone might take it before she found it, and we need to get it to her before her grandmother's birthday tomorrow.

Jane: Why did I ever spend that money? I hate these shorts.

Mandy: I'll go with you to Angela's. It's my fault too. I could have told her you found the wallet, but I didn't.

Jane: You were just being a good friend. I'm the one to blame. Come on. Let's ask Mom to take us to Angela's house. I'll feel a lot better when I return her wallet and the money.

(*They exit, then reenter with Mother.*)

Jane: Angela sure has a swell family. They weren't even mad at me.

Mandy: Angela was so happy to get that money, she cried.

Mother: I'm proud of you girls. You admitted making a mistake and corrected it. We all make mistakes. Correcting them gives us a chance to start over right.

Jane: I feel a lot better now, even though it will be a while before I get a pair of roller skates. My stomachache is gone. Let's all have some chocolate chip cookies.

Mother: Chocolate chip cookies, huh? Now I *know* everything is back to normal!

(*All exit.*)

April

Forgiving Is an Easter Thing to Do

Theme: Forgiveness
Scripture: Matthew 6:12
Characters: Tim, John, Chuck, Ralph

Note: This script may be used in March and March's "Aren't Finders Keepers?" used in April should Easter fall in March.

Tim: No, no, no.

John: Be reasonable.

Tim: I won't do it.

John: If you don't, who will?

Tim: Who cares?

John: But you're the one who tripped Ralph and made him sprain
        his ankle. You're the only one who can run in his place.

Tim: What do you mean I made Ralph trip?

John: I saw you. When he ran by, you stuck out your foot, and he
        tripped over it.

Tim: I did not.

John: You did too.

Tim: Well, he was acting so big and smart, I thought he needed to
        come down a notch.

John: Look at the fine mess it put us in. We could easily win that
        relay race against Preston Elementary with Ralph. Without
        Ralph, we're short our best player—unless you help us.

Tim: But, John, I can't do that. I used to go to Preston. I don't want
        to compete against them.

John: I get it. You tripped Ralph so Preston could win.

Tim: No, no! I go to Hope Elementary now. I want Hope to win.

John: Then join our relay team.

Tim: I can't. It would be like turning traitor.

John: You're either for Hope or against us. There's no two ways
        about it.

Tim: I'm for Hope, but I'm for Preston too.

John: You can't have it both ways. Either you play for Hope's team,
        or I tell the other kids you tripped Ralph on purpose.

Tim: You wouldn't!

John: Yes, I would. I'll be back in a little while to get your decision.
        (*Exits.*)

Tim: What am I going to do?

Chuck (*enters*):   Hi, Tim. What's wrong?

Tim: John says I have to play on the Hope relay team. But that
        would mean I'd have to compete against Preston, and I used to
        go there.

Chuck: You're in a fix.

Tim: It's all my fault. I should never have tripped Ralph.

Chuck: You tripped Ralph?

Tim: Uh, no . . . no, of course not. I said I never should have skipped south. You know, gone from Preston, which is north, to Hope, which is south.

Chuck: Are you sure you didn't say you tripped Ralph?

Tim: Of course I'm sure. What kind of creep would trip Ralph?

Chuck: I don't know. Everyone likes Ralph.

Tim: Maybe he tripped over a stone or something.

Ralph (*enters hobbling*):   Hi, guys.

Chuck: How's your foot?

Ralph: Too sore and swollen to run in the relay race.

Tim: That's too bad.

Chuck: How did you fall, Ralph?

Ralph: I tripped over something.

Tim: Like a stone, maybe.

Ralph: Maybe.

Chuck: Like a foot, maybe?

Ralph: More like a stone.

Chuck: Oh. Well, I've got to go. Hope you get well soon, Ralph. (*Exits.*)

Tim: You knew I tripped you all the time, didn't you?

Ralph: Yeah, I knew.

Tim: Why didn't you tell on me?

Ralph: I thought about it. At first I was really mad at you. Then I remembered that Jesus died, carrying all my sins and all your sins, and that He loves us both the same.

Tim: Jesus died for *my* sins? Even for tripping you?

Ralph: Yeah. He died for everyone's sins. You know all about that, don't you?

Tim: Oh, uh, sure. I heard it somewhere before.

Ralph: Don't you go to church anywhere?

Tim: Nah. My folks think church is for sissies. But I don't think you're a sissy.

Ralph: Thanks, pal.

Tim: You're calling me your pal after I tripped you?

Ralph: Sure. God forgave you for all your sins, so why shouldn't I?

Tim: Gosh. I've never heard anything like this before.

Ralph: Maybe I'm feeling bighearted because it's Easter time, and our Sunday School teacher was reminding us about how much

God loves us. Maybe you're lucky. If you had tripped me in January, maybe I would have given you a knuckle sandwich.

Tim: Whew! I'm glad it's Easter.

Ralph: I don't know what to do about the race. I really wanted to run.

Tim: I'll run for you.

Ralph: But you'd have to run against Preston, your old school.

Tim: I know. It will be tough. But you've been swell to me. I figure I should repay you.

Ralph: You don't have to repay me.

Tim: You mean I don't have to run for you? Even if I don't repay you, you'll still forgive me?

Ralph: I've already forgiven you, silly.

Tim: You have?

Ralph: Yes. You just have to believe it.

Tim: OK. I guess I believe it.

Ralph: That's good enough for a start.

Tim: You know, going to Preston was swell, and I had some good friends there. But I'm going to Hope now. Maybe I should support Hope.

Ralph: Only you can decide that.

Tim: John told me I had to run for Hope or he'd tell everyone I tripped you.

Ralph: Don't let John upset you. I'll stand up for you.

Tim: Wow. You're something else.

Ralph: I'm just grateful to my friend, Jesus, for standing up for me. When I do something wrong, He reminds God that He died for my sins and that I'm forgiven.

Tim: That settles it.

Ralph: What settles what?

Tim: I'm definitely going to run for you in the relay race.

Ralph: That's swell. What made you decide to do it?

Tim: You didn't pressure me. You just forgave me even though I tripped you.

Ralph: Thanks, pal.

John (*enters*):   Hi, Ralph. I didn't expect to see you here.

Ralph: Hi.

John: Did you make your decision, Tim?

Tim: Yeah. But before I tell you what it is, Ralph knows I tripped him.

John: He does?

Ralph: Tim's my friend.

John: He is?

Ralph: Sure. He's a swell guy. You'll like him once you get to know him too.

John: What about the relay race?

Tim: I'll run for Hope.

John: You will?

Tim: Sure. I figure I can race against Preston Elementary and still be friends with the people who go there.

Ralph: I've got to go. Happy Easter. (*Exits.*)

Tim: Yeah, happy Easter.

John: Happy Easter?! What's that got to do with relay races?

Tim: Come on. I'll explain it to you.

(*Both exit.*)

April

April Showers Bring May Flowers

Theme: Judging Others
Scripture: Matthew 7:1-2
Characters: Ginger, Hazel, Cynthia, Jimmy, Paul

Ginger: I've got a terrible problem.

Hazel: What is it?

Ginger: I don't know who to invite to my birthday party.

Hazel: Invite the whole class.

Ginger: If I do, the new boys, Paul and Jimmy, will come, and Cynthia says they're really mean.

Hazel: Then don't invite them.

Ginger: If I don't, they'll hate me.

Hazel: So what?

Ginger: So what?! Don't you remember what Paul and Jimmy did to Cynthia when she didn't invite them to her party?

Hazel: Yeah. She said they put bubblegum in her hair and she had to get it cut. What are you worried about? Your hair is already short.

Ginger: Thanks a lot! I'd probably have to shave my head!

Hazel (*laughs*): That would be a riot.

Ginger: You're no help.

Hazel: Why not have it on a day Paul and Jimmy can't come?

Ginger: They can *always* come.

Hazel: Then tell them you sent them an invitation but it got lost in the mail.

Ginger: I can't do that. That would be telling a lie.

Hazel: Isn't that better than the bubblegum treatment?

Ginger: I don't know. If I had my birthday in the summer instead of in April, I wouldn't have to invite the whole class. Why are there so many problems when you try to plan something nice? My parents are even having trouble getting the clown to come and entertain us.

Hazel: You know what they say. April showers bring May flowers.

Ginger: You cornball.

Hazel: You could skip your birthday party.

Ginger: You've got to be kidding. That would be no fun at all.

Hazel: Then you'd better invite Paul and Jimmy unless you want bubblegum in your hair.

Ginger: That sure was a mean thing they did to Cynthia.

Hazel: They say they didn't put the bubblegum in her hair, but nobody believes them. Nobody even likes them.

Ginger: Maybe if I invite them, they'll feel like somebody likes them. Anyway, the Bible says to love our neighbors as ourselves, and I guess that means Jimmy and Paul.

Hazel: It's your party.

(*Both exit, then reenter.*)

Ginger: Hazel, the whole class is in my living room, even Jimmy and Paul. Can you believe they all came?

Hazel: That's great. Look at all your presents.

Ginger: I know. I'll bet Jimmy and Paul brought me something gross like a dead mouse.

Hazel: Maybe not. They're sitting real quiet on the sofa, like they're uncomfortable. They don't look very mean to me.

Ginger: Why do I have to worry about problems like what they're up to on my birthday? It isn't fair to have to think about things like that. I wish I hadn't invited them.

Hazel: Quit worrying. Did your parents get that clown to come perform?

Ginger: No, he couldn't come.

Hazel: Too bad. Everybody was looking forward to that.

Ginger: How come? You were the only one who knew we were trying to get him.

Hazel: Well, I got so excited about it, I told Cynthia. And you know Cynthia. She told everyone.

Ginger: You and your big mouth. Now I have to tell them he isn't coming. More problems!

Hazel: I'm sorry, Ginger.

(*Cynthia enters.*)

Cynthia: Hi, you two. Making final party plans in the kitchen? I'm dying to see the clown. When is he coming?

Ginger: There is no clown.

Cynthia: But Hazel told me there was going to be one.

Hazel: And you told everyone else.

Cynthia: If you didn't want me to tell, you should have told me it was a secret. And Ginger, why did you invite those two terrible boys?

Ginger: Jimmy and Paul?

Cynthia: Yeah, the bubblegum freaks.

Ginger: They've behaved themselves just fine so far.

Cynthia: Don't hold your breath. (*Exits.*)

(*Jimmy and Paul enter, acting shy.*)

Jimmy: Cynthia says there won't be a clown.

Ginger: That's right. Please don't get mad, boys.

Hazel: Yeah, please don't do anything mean.

Paul: We came to help.

Ginger and Hazel: You did?

Jimmy: If you'll let us use your mom's lipstick and a couple of wigs, we'll be the clowns.

Hazel (*aside to Ginger*): That might keep them out of trouble.

Ginger: OK, boys. Come with me. I'll get you what you need.

(*Ginger, Jimmy, and Paul exit. Cynthia enters.*)

Cynthia: I'll bet those two boys were so mad there was no clown that they put bubblegum in Ginger's hair.

Hazel: No, they didn't.

Cynthia: Well, she's lucky. That's all I can say.

Hazel: How's the party going?

Cynthia: Dull. Everyone's disappointed about the clown.

Hazel: Let's go see if we can liven up the party.

(*Hazel and Cynthia exit. Jimmy and Paul enter in clown getup. Ginger also enters.*)

Ginger: You boys look like a scream. It's really nice of you to help me out like this.

Jimmy: We like to clown around.

Paul: Do you think they'll recognize us?

Ginger: I don't know. You sure don't look like yourselves. Get out there and see.

(*Jimmy and Paul exit. Hazel enters.*)

Hazel: Ginger, those boys are a scream. They have everyone laughing so hard they're holding their sides.

Ginger: And to think I almost didn't invite them.

Hazel: We were sure wrong about them.

Ginger: I know. Cynthia was always talking about how mean they are, so I thought they'd be awful.

Hazel: Even Cynthia's laughing. She doesn't recognize them.

Ginger: I think it's time to serve the cake and punch now that everyone's in a good mood.

Hazel: OK, I'll get some of the girls to help. (*Exits.*)

Ginger: This birthday party is turning out OK after all.

(*Hazel and Cynthia reenter.*)

Cynthia: This is simply awful! There's bubblegum in my hair again.

Ginger: That's terrible. What happened?

Cynthia: Someone put it in my hair. It must have been Jimmy and Paul. They snuck up on me.

Hazel: It couldn't have been them. They were clear across the room from you.

Cynthia: I didn't see them.

Hazel: They were the clowns.

Cynthia: Those awful boys? Impossible!

Ginger: But they were.

Cynthia: Then who put the gum in my hair?

Hazel: You did.

Cynthia: How dare you!

Hazel: When I served you cake, you took the gum out of your mouth and put it behind your ear.

Cynthia: I did?

Hazel: Yeah. And I'll bet that's what happened the last time you had gum in your hair and blamed it on Paul and Jimmy.

Cynthia: You're terrible, and I'm sorry I ever came to this party.

Ginger: Don't be mad. We still like you. My mom will help you get the gum out of your hair. She's good at that sort of thing. Just go down the hall.

(*Cynthia exits. Jimmy and Paul enter in clown getups.*)

Jimmy: They thought we were funny.

Paul: They liked us, even when they found out who we were.

Ginger: You saved my birthday party. I'm really glad I invited you. You're swell guys.

Jimmy and Paul: Thanks. (*They exit.*)

Ginger: My problem party turned into a blessing for lots of people.

Hazel: See, I told you April showers bring May flowers.

(*Ginger and Hazel exit.*)

May

The Graduation Party

Theme: Responsibility
Scripture: Proverbs 20:4
Characters: Jill, Jane, Holly, Holly's Mother

Jill: Why are you sweeping that dirt under the rug?

Jane: Because it's easier than going to the hall closet to get the dustpan.

Jill: But Mom told us to clean up our room.

Jane: I am. Look. The floor's clean.

Jill: Except under the rug.

Jane: Who cares? It looks clean.

Jill: I give up. Did you empty the trash?

Jane: Yeah.

Jill: Where'd you put it?

Jane: In the kitchen garbage can.

Jill: But you're supposed to put it in the trash can outside.

Jane: What's the diff? It all gets emptied.

Jill: Now Mom will have to empty the kitchen trash sooner.

Jane: She doesn't mind. That's her job anyway.

Jill: You're something else. (*Pauses.*) Did you get an invitation to Holly's graduation party?

Jane: Yeah. Big deal. So she's graduating from third grade. So are you, but you're not making a production out of it.

Jill: I'm going. Are you?

Jane: I might.

Jill: You're supposed to call and tell her whether you're going by tonight.

Jane: Oh, yeah. I forgot. This RSVP stuff sure is dumb.

Jill: How do you expect her to plan the party if she doesn't know how many people are coming?

Jane: She can guess. Anyway, knowing how many isn't that important. If I have a third grade graduation party next year, I'll invite everyone. And they won't have to RSVP.

Jill: You're impossible.

(*Jill and Jane exit. Holly and her mother enter.*)

Holly: Thirty-six people said they're coming to my party, Mom. Last night was the last night to RSVP. So now we can really start planning.

Mother: Wonderful. The party's only three days away. We'd better get busy.

Holly: First, we need to bake twelve pies. If we cut them into six pieces each, that will be enough for everyone to have two pieces. Then we'll make popcorn balls and buy ice cream and get thirty-six party favors from the store. And we'll make name tags and hats with each person's name on his own. Then we can plan all our games around the hats and name tags, and they'll have something to take home as a keepsake from the party.

Mother: Whew! I'm glad you only graduate from third grade once.

Holly: Me too. I'd hate to repeat it. I'd probably get Mrs. Flaxon again and have to put up with her "I *said* get to *work*, students."

Mother: Is everyone from both your school and Sunday School classes coming?

Holly: Yeah. Everyone except Jane. I wonder if I did something to make her mad. Maybe she forgot to RSVP.

Mother: Want to remind her?

Holly: No, I don't think so. If she didn't want to come, she might think I was trying to make her, and she'd be uncomfortable.

Mother: Okay, honey. It's your party. (*Both exit.*)

(*Jill and Jane enter.*)

Jill: I'm so excited. Tonight is Holly's graduation party, and I can hardly wait. I know it will be fun.

Jane: Tonight's the party? Yikes! I forgot all about it.

Jill: Didn't you tell her you were coming?

Jane: No.

Jill: That means you can't go.

Jane: Why not? Just because I forgot to RSVP, so what?

Jill: She's only planning for the ones who called. I know, because when I talked to her a couple of days ago, she told me everything she's planning to do.

Jane: That's ridiculous. I'm sure she's planning for a few people who forgot to tell her they were coming.

Jill: Oh, brother! If you go, you'll embarrass Holly and yourself.

Jane: Baloney.

Jill: Don't say I didn't warn you. (*Both exit.*)

(*Jill and Jane enter.*)

Jill: Knock, knock.

Holly (*enters*): Hi, Jill. Here's your hat with your very own name on it. And here's your name tag.

Jane: Hi, Holly.

Holly: Oh, uh, Jane. Hi. I didn't think you were coming. I don't have a name tag or a hat for you.

Jane: That's OK.

Holly: Uh, all our games are related to the hats and name tags.

Jane: Just put me with the others who forgot to tell you they were coming.

Holly: Sorry, Jane, but you're the only one.

Jane: Oh.

Holly: I hate to turn you away, Jane, but I hate to ruin the game plans too. And I know you wouldn't be happy sitting in the corner just watching.

Jane: But I want to stay at the party. I didn't forget to RSVP on purpose, Holly. Please let me stay.

Holly: Well, if you stay, we could put you to work helping to serve refreshments.

Jane: You've got to be kidding. I don't want to stay at any dumb party where I have to serve refreshments.

Jill: Just go, Jane, and don't make a scene.

Jane: I'm going, I'm going. Who wants to attend your dumb party anyway? Graduating from third grade is a stupid reason to have a party. And RSVPs are stupid too. (*She stomps out.*)

(*Holly and Jill exit. Jill and Jane enter.*)

Jane (*sarcastically*):   Did you have a good time at the party?

Jill: Wonderful! I won a door prize, a huge eraser.

Jane: You know what I'd do what that eraser?

Jill: What?

Jane: Take it to all the stores that sell RSVP cards and erase all the RSVPs.

Jill: What a baby you are!

Jane: I suppose everyone knew Holly made me leave the party.

Jill: No. She didn't tell anyone, and neither did I. When people asked where you were, we just said you had to be someplace else.

Jane: Oh.

Jill: Holly sent something home for you.

Jane: Whatever it is, I don't want it.

Jill: Not even a piece of chocolate pie with thick meringue on top? I put it in the fridge for you.

Jane: How dumb! A chocolate pie instead of a cake. People who make big deals about graduating are sure silly.

Jill: You're the one who's making a big deal about something silly. So you forgot to RSVP and couldn't go to the party. So what? You made a mistake. Learn from it.

Jane: You sound just like an adult. Learn from it, learn from it. What if I don't want to learn from it?

Jill: It's your life. (*Exits.*)

Jane: Yeah, it's my life. And the first thing I'm going to do with it is eat that chocolate pie. (*Exits and reenters quickly in a rage.*) Where's my chocolate pie?

Jill (*enters*): I ate it. You said you didn't want it.

Jane: I don't believe it. Nothing's going right. Even my own sister hates me.

Jill: I don't hate you. But you *said* you didn't want your pie.

Jane: You and your talk about being responsible. If you were responsible, you would have left my pie alone.

Jill: If you were responsible, you would have told Holly you were coming. Then you could have had two pieces of pie.

Jane: Nobody's being fair to me.

Jill: You're the one who sweeps dirt under the rug, empties garbage into other people's garbage cans, and crashes parties. If everyone acted like you do, the whole world would be in a huge mess. (*Exits.*)

Jane: Ah, what does she know? The world's already in a huge mess. I didn't get to go to the party or eat my chocolate pie. (*Sighs.*) Maybe I could have done something a little different. I'll have to think about that.

(*She exits.*)

May

Mother's Day

Theme: Respect for Mothers
Scripture: Exodus 20:12
Characters: Lucy, Bob, Mother, Father

Lucy: Oh, no, look what day it is.

Bob: I don't have to look. It's Sunday.

Lucy: I know, silly. But it's only a week until Mother's Day.

Bob: So?

Lucy: So, what are we going to do for Mom on Mother's Day?

Bob: I don't know. Maybe she'll make herself a cake.

Lucy: Bob!

Bob (*mockingly*): Lucy!

Lucy: It's not fair for her to make her own Mother's Day cake.
        Anyway, I don't think she's that wild about cake.

Bob: She's wild about it, all right. She just doesn't like the calories.

Lucy: That rules out a box of candy, then.

Bob: Wait a minute. We could get her the candy, then eat it for her.

Lucy: Some help you are.

Bob: Yep. I always help myself to anything I can.

Lucy: Older brothers are supposed to be an inspiration. You're
        nothing but a blob.

Bob: A blob?

Lucy: Yeah. Blobby Bob.

Bob: And you're fruity Lucy.

Lucy: That's it!

Bob: What's it?

Lucy: Fruit. We can get her fruit for Mother's Day.

Bob: She could buy that herself. We ought to get her something she
        can't get for herself.

Lucy: Oh. That's a tall order.

Bob: We're smart. We'll think of something.

Lucy: We could give her breakfast in bed.

Bob: I guess so. We did that last year, anyway.

Lucy: Yeah, and Dad had to clean up the kitchen.

Bob: I remember. He kept mumbling about marmalade in the
        toaster. Maybe we'd better do something different this year.

Lucy: Like what?

Bob: Maybe we could draw her some pictures.

Lucy: OK. Let's go to our room and get some paper and crayons.

Bob: Good idea. We'll draw her lots of neat pictures about what
        happened during the year.

(Bob and Lucy exit. Mother and Father enter.)

Mother: Whew! I'm glad Thursday's over. It's been hectic. The kids'

room was a mess. They had paper strewn all over. It took me
forever to clean it up.

Father: You really shouldn't clean up for them, honey. They've got
to learn to keep their own room neat.

Mother: I know I shouldn't. But it gets so messy I can't stand it.
Then I just have to do something.

(*Both exit. Lucy and Bob enter.*)

Lucy: Bob, something terrible has happened!

Bob: What?

Lucy: Our Mother's Day pictures are gone.

Bob: Are you sure?

Lucy: I'm sure. Remember how we left them on the floor?

Bob: Yeah.

Lucy: Well, there's nothing on the floor, and it looks like somebody
swept it.

Bob: Uh-oh. Mother's been cleaning again.

Lucy: It's all your fault.

Bob: My fault?!

Lucy: Yes. You were supposed to clean the room last weekend, and
you didn't sweep or anything.

Bob: Wait just a big fat minute. You were supposed to clean up the
weekend before that, and *you* didn't do it. Why should I clean
up when you don't?

Lucy: Because. You're older. That's why.

Bob: Don't give me that garbage.

Lucy: Now what are we going to do? It took us four days to draw
all those pictures. We'll never get them all drawn again by Sunday.

Bob: We'll just have to give her something else.

Lucy: But what? My brains are all thought out.

Bob: It will have to be something that won't take long.

Lucy: You know what Sandra is doing for her mother?

Bob: No.

Lucy: She's giving her a jar full of little slips of paper that say things
like "Good for washing dishes one meal" and "Good for tidying
the living room." When her mother doesn't have time to do one
of those things, she pulls one out, and Sandra does it for her as
a Mother's Day present all year long.

Bob: I don't like the sound of that. We could get pretty busy if Mom
pulled out very many slips of paper.

Lucy: Yeah, I suppose so.

Bob: Anyway, we wouldn't have time to write down all those things before Sunday.

Lucy: You're right. It took Sandra a week. She wrote fifty slips of paper.

Bob: Fifty! She must love hard work. Maybe we can buy Mom a card and write inside it something we promise to do for her.

Lucy: Like what?

Bob: I don't know. Like, uh, like clean up our room every week.

Lucy: We're already supposed to do that.

Bob: I know. But we don't.

Lucy: That's true. And if we did, maybe Mom wouldn't throw away our stuff by mistake. But we both have to promise to do it or it won't work.

Bob: I promise.

Lucy: Do you think that's enough of a present?

Bob: Well, I don't think Mom likes to cook very well.

Lucy: I know. Maybe we could fix her breakfast in bed once a month if Dad will help us clean up.

Bob: Uh, well, I don't think Dad will go for that. He talked about marmalade in the toaster and the broken egg in the bottom of the fridge for weeks after Mother's Day was over last year.

Lucy: I didn't mean to drop it. It just slid out of my hand. Then I forgot to clean it up.

Bob: Maybe the part about cleaning up our room will be enough.

Lucy: Yeah.

Bob: We sure thought of a different present, didn't we?

Lucy: We sure did. I can hardly wait to see Mom's face when she opens the card Sunday.

(*Lucy and Bob exit. Father and Mother enter.*)

Father: Happy Mother's Day.

Mother: Thanks. I have to admit I'm really relieved the kids didn't fix me breakfast in bed.

Father: I wonder what they're up to this year?

Mother: Who knows?

(*Bob and Lucy enter.*)

Lucy: Happy Mother's Day.

Bob: Yeah. Happy Mother's Day.

Mother: Thanks, children. I love you both.

Lucy: Yeah, I know. Because without us, you wouldn't be a mother, right?

Mother: How'd you get so smart?

Lucy: Because I inherited your brains.

Mother: Then you've got to be brilliant.

Bob: Here's our Mother's Day present.

Lucy: It doesn't look like much, but open it.

Mother: A card! How nice. Let's see what it says inside. "Dear Mom, we promise to keep our room clean all year. Love, Bob and Lucy."

Lucy: Do you like it?

Mother: I love it! That's the nicest Mother's Day present you've ever given me.

Father: And I'll check to make sure you keep your promise.

Lucy and Bob: Don't worry. We will.

Father: Now it's my turn to give you a present.

Mother: OK.

Father: Here it is.

Mother: A box of chocolates! You really shouldn't have.

Father: But I love you—and I love chocolates, too.

Mother: So that's why you bought them. You figured you'd get them all because I'm trying to count calories.

Bob: You don't have to worry about getting fat. I'll help you eat them.

Lucy: Me, too.

Mother: Maybe I'll have just one.

Bob: Mmmm! This candy is yummy. I love Mother's Day!

(*All exit.*)

June

Father's Day

Theme: Being Chosen
Scripture: Matthew 22:14
Characters: Tommy, Stan, Tina, Mrs. Walker

Stan: Hi, Tommy. Are you going to the Father's Day picnic at the park?

Tommy: Hi, Stan. I sure am.

Stan: I'd like to meet your dad. Is he really six feet five?

Tommy: Yep. All he has to do is reach his hand up a little ways and he can touch the ceiling.

Stan: Wow! That must be neat.

Tommy: It is, unless he runs into low doorways.

Stan: Ouch!

Tommy: You get the picture.

Stan: If your Dad's so tall, how come you're so short? Is your Mom short?

Tommy: No, she's almost six feet tall.

Stan: You must have some short uncles or aunts then.

Tommy: Nope. Everyone's tall.

Stan: Well, how come you aren't?

Tommy: Because, silly, I'm adopted.

Stan (*embarrassed*):   Oh.

Tommy: Don't be embarrassed. I think it's great to be adopted.

Stan: You do?

Tommy: Sure. See, my Mom and Dad got to see me before they decided they wanted me. They could have said, not him, we'll wait for another one to come along. But they didn't. They said he's the one we want, and they took me home.

Stan: Doesn't it bother you not to know who your real parents are?

Tommy: Sometimes I wonder who they were. I figure they were probably short. But I also figure my real parents are the ones who chose me.

Stan: I guess that's pretty neat, to be chosen.

Tommy: I think so. I *know* my Mom and Dad want me.

Stan: My parents want me, too. They told me all about how they planned for me.

Tommy: See, we were all chosen one way or another.

Stan: You sound just like Mrs. Walker in Sunday School. Remember how she said last Sunday that we're all chosen?

Tommy: Do I ever! That was when Tina said, "You're chosen to stand on your head."

Stan: And you said, "You're chosen to sit on your face."

Tommy: And everyone laughed except Mrs. Walker.

Stan: That was fun. I wish we could have that class over again.

Tommy: Why don't we? Let's pretend we're back there.

Stan: OK.

(*Both exit. Enter Stan, Tom, Mrs. Walker, and Tina.*)

Mrs. Walker: Today we're going to talk about being chosen. Have any of you ever been chosen for something?

Stan: I was chosen to play Joseph in the Christmas play.

Tina: I was chosen to have the picture I drew in school hung on the wall because it was the best one.

Tommy: I was chosen to take out the trash.

Mrs. Walker: Don't feel lonely. I was chosen to do that a few times too. We've all been chosen to do something at some time or other.

Tina (*to Tommy*):   You're chosen to stand on your head.

Tommy (*to Tina*):   You're chosen to sit on your face.

Mrs. Walker: Children, let's not forget where we are.

Tommy: I know. In God's house.

Mrs. Walker: That's right. And speaking of God, there is someone who has chosen all of us.

Stan: Who?

Mrs. Walker: Can any of you guess?

Tommy: Uncle Sam.

Tina: The Pied Piper.

Mrs. Walker: God has chosen all of us. Do you know why?

Stan: No.

Mrs. Walker: Because He wants you to be His sons and daughters. He loves you all. Just as your own fathers love you, except He loves you even more.

Tommy: My dad loves me a lot. He bought me a toy train.

Tina: My dad loves me, too. He let me have the last helping of chocolate ice cream even though he wanted it, and he fixed my doll's broken arm.

Stan: My dad took me to a baseball game.

Mrs. Walker: Your dads want what's best for you, don't they?

Tommy: Yeah.

Mrs. Walker: God wants what's best for you too. He knows what's best for you, and He hopes you'll choose those things. But He doesn't make you. He's chosen you to have all sorts of blessings, but you have to obey His will to get them.

Stan: I knew there was a catch to it.

Mrs. Walker: It's a little like your parents. I'll bet your dads have

told you something like, if you clean your room, we'll go to a
movie tonight.

(*All three agree.*)

Mrs. Walker: You had to do what you were asked before you got the
prize, didn't you?

Tommy: Yep.

Mrs. Walker: That's like God. He has chosen you to do some important things for Him. Each of you has something special that God
has called you to do. If you do it, you'll get the prize.

Tommy: What's the prize?

Tina: The blessings of God, silly.

Mrs. Walker: God wants everyone to have His blessings. He consid-
ers everyone His children, but not everyone accepts Him as
their father. That makes Him sad.

Tina: You mean I'm God's daughter, and Stan and Tommy are his
sons?

Mrs. Walker: That's right. I'm His daughter too. We're all chosen to
be His children. But if you don't choose to let Him be your father
and to obey Him, He can't bless you as He wants to.

Tina: I get it. It's kind of like with my dad. Yesterday he told me
if I didn't help Mom clean up the living room, we couldn't go to
the zoo.

Stan: That *is* what my dad told me yesterday. We went to the zoo,
but I didn't see you there.

Tina: That's because I didn't clean up the living room. I was too
busy playing with my doll.

Tommy: Aha! You were called, but you chose not to be chosen.

Stan: Shame on you.

Mrs. Walker: We all make mistakes like that. But God calls us again
and again, hoping we'll choose Him.

(*Bell rings.*)

Mrs. Walker: Oops, end of class. Don't forget the Father's Day
picnic next week, kids. Why don't you all choose to bring your
fathers?

(*All four exit. Tommy and Stan reappear.*)

Tommy: That was a pretty neat class.

Stan: Yeah. I think it's super that God chose all of us to be His kids.
It's like your parents choosing you to be their kid.

Tommy: I think so too. And now I'm choosing to take my dad to the
Father's Day picnic.

Stan: I'll go home and tell my dad I choose to take him too.

Tommy: OK. Oops, I'd better get home fast. At our house if we don't get home for supper on time, we get chosen to take out the trash.

Stan: You better hustle! See you at the picnic.

(*Both exit.*)

June

A Cure for Boring Summers

Theme: Helping Others
Scripture: Matthew 25:40
Characters: Gail, Kathy, Mrs. Harris

Gail: I thought it would be so great getting out of school. But now I'm bored.

Kathy: I know what you mean. I've been rollerskating, jumping rope, and playing hopscotch and all sorts of games for two weeks. Now I'm ready to do something else.

Gail: Me, too. What shall we do?

Kathy: We could go down to the police station and talk to Officer Stewart. He always has candy in his pockets for kids.

Gail: He's on vacation this week.

Kathy: Oh. We could try talking our parents into taking us on a picnic.

Gail: OK. If we all go together, we'll *really* have fun.

Kathy: Let's ask our folks if we can go.

(*They exit, then reenter.*)

Kathy: My folks said no. What did your folks say?

Gail: The same thing. They're too busy with chores around the house to go on a picnic.

Kathy: What lousy luck! Now what are we going to do?

Gail: I don't know. I guess we could sit on the porch and watch people go by.

Kathy: That's what *old* people do.

Gail: But it's kind of fun. A couple of days ago I saw Bobby Reynolds fly by on his roller skates, showing off, as usual. He hit a crack and landed kerplunk on his seat. It was funny.

Kathy: You mean Bobby, the cute kid from school?

Gail: Yeah. But I think he's a brat.

Kathy: Let's sit on the porch a while. Maybe he'll come back again.

Gail: Have you got a crush on that creep?

Kathy: He's not a creep. I think he's adorable.

Gail: Oh, brother!

(*Both exit, then reenter.*)

Gail: We've been sitting here twenty minutes, and I haven't seen Bobby or any other kids around.

Kathy: Look at Mrs. Harris. It looks like she's trying to pull weeds.

Gail: She keeps holding her back.

Kathy: It probably hurts.

Gail: Maybe we should help her weed her flower bed.

Kathy: I guess we could. There's nothing better to do.

Gail: I'll race you across the street to her house.

Kathy: Watch out for cars.

(*They run across the stage. Mrs. Harris enters.*)

Gail: Hi, Mrs. Harris. What are you doing?

Mrs. Harris: Hello, Gail. I'm trying to weed my garden. But my rheumatism is acting up today.

Kathy: We'll help you weed your garden.

Mrs. Harris: I couldn't ask you to do that. It's hard work, and this is your vacation from school.

Kathy: But we're bored.

Gail: It would be fun to help you weed your flower bed.

Mrs. Harris: How nice of you. There are petunias, marigolds, nasturtiums, pansies, and snapdragons growing here. Pull anything that doesn't look like one of them.

Gail: OK.

Kathy: We'll finish this in a flash. You go inside and rest awhile.

Mrs. Harris: You're such lovely girls.

(*Mrs. Harris exits, then reenters.*)

Mrs. Harris: You've been working half an hour, girls. Don't you think it's time for a break?

Gail: We're all finished. Kathy just pulled the last weed.

Mrs. Harris: My, my. You're such good workers. Come in and have some chocolate chip cookies and orange juice.

Gail: Yum!

(*All three exit. Gail and Kathy reenter.*)

Kathy: That was sure fun yesterday, helping Mrs. Harris.

Gail: And eating her delicious cookies.

Kathy: Let's see who we can help today.

Gail: OK. Mom told me yesterday that Mr. Thomas's wife is in the hospital. Maybe we could help him clean his house.

Kathy: OK. And Miss Davis who's in a wheelchair, a couple of blocks away, needs someone to do her grocery shopping.

Gail: We can do that.

Kathy: At this rate, we won't be bored for the rest of the summer.

Gail: This is almost as much fun as going on a picnic.

Kathy: We can still do that. Mom and Dad said that we could go tomorrow and that I could bring a friend. Want to come?

Gail: I'd love to. But now let's visit Mr. Thomas. I'll bet his house is a mess.

Kathy: OK, but I'll bet he won't have any chocolate chip cookies to give us.

Gail: You goof! If he doesn't have any, we'll make him some.

Kathy: And I'll ask my folks if we can invite him on our picnic.
Gail: Great idea.
(*Both exit.*)

July

Independence Day

Theme: Freedom
Scripture: John 8:36
Characters: Julie, Jan

Julie (*singsongy*): Today I'm independent. Today I'm independent. Today I'm. . . .

Jan: What are you so happy about?

Julie: Because. (*Sings again.*) Today I'm independent, today I'm . . . .

Jan: Big deal. How come you're all of a sudden so independent?

Julie: Because Mom and Dad told me that today is Independence Day, and I'm independent.

Jan: Independent from what?

Julie: I don't know. I'm just independent.

Jan: If you don't know what you're independent from, you're no better off than you were yesterday.

Julie: I am too better off.

Jan: You are not.

Julie: I am too.

Jan: Are not.

Julie: Am too. I'll tell you why. You know the Indy 500, that famous car race?

Jan: Of course. Everyone knows about that.

Julie: Well, I'm part of the Indy Pendant.

Jan: What's that supposed to mean?

Julie: You've never heard of the Indy Pendant?!

Jan (*defensively*): No.

Julie: Instead of racing five hundred miles, we race to see how long it takes to make a pendant.

Jan: A what?

Julie: A pendant. You know. Like a necklace.

Jan: You're crazy. No wonder I never heard of the Indy Pendant. There is no such thing.

Julie: How would you know?

Jan: Because nothing could be that stupid. And I happen to know today is Independence Day. It's a celebration of the day the United States got its freedom from Great Britain.

Julie: See? I know why I'm independent. Because we're free from the British.

Jan: You only know that because I just told you.

Julie: You think you're so smart.

Jan: I am.

Julie: Such conceit!

Jan: I also know that tonight at the fireworks they're going to shoot off a whole bunch of starbursts.

Julie: Oh, boy! I love starbursts. How many will they shoot?

Jan: About twenty-five.

Julie: Wow! I'm going. Are you?

Jan: I wouldn't miss it for anything.

Julie: If you're so smart, tell me why we shoot firecrackers off every Independence Day.

Jan: That's easy. Because when the American settlers fought the British, they used cannons and muskets and things that sound like firecrackers. So we celebrate Independence Day with firecrackers.

Julie: I give up. How did you get so smart?

Jan: From listening to Mom and Dad talk and from reading encyclopedias.

Julie: You read encyclopedias?!

Jan: Yeah.

Julie: How boring. I read comic books.

Jan: You may think reading encyclopedias is boring, but I knew what Independence Day was, and you didn't.

Julie: So what? I'm still independent.

Jan: What will you do with your independence?

Julie: I think I'll build a raft and float down the river.

Jan: Dumbhead! You can't build a raft.

Julie: OK, then, I'll get one of the sticks hobos carry, put a bandana on the end, pack some food, clothes, and my kitten in it, and go hiking across the country for a while.

Jan: Think your Mom and Dad will let you?

Julie: They told me I was independent. That means I can do anything I want to.

Jan: OK. Then do it. But don't call me if you get lost.

Julie: Lost?

Jan: Yeah, or some mean person hurts you.

Julie: Really? Did you learn that by reading those encyclopedias?

Jan: No. I learned it on TV.

Julie: If I can't go rafting or hoboing on Independence Day, what's the use of having Independence Day at all?

Jan: Because it helps us remember to be thankful for our free country.

Julie: What's free about it if I can't go rafting or hoboing?

Jan: You can go. But you'll have to learn to build and sail a raft and how to stay away from mean people and not get lost.

Julie: Those sound kind of hard. Maybe I'll just watch the firecrack-
         ers.

Jan: Did you go to school last year?

Julie: Of course, silly. I sat behind you in class.

Jan: You know how many countries there are where kids can't go
         to school if they want to?

Julie: Lots, I suppose.

Jan: That's right.

Julie: Here, I have to go to school even if I don't want to. I might
         like to live someplace where I don't have to go to school.

Jan: Then you wouldn't know how to read.

Julie: So?

Jan: You couldn't read comic books any more.

Julie: I forgot about them.

Jan: You know how many countries there are where you can't go
         to church if you want to?

Julie: How many?

Jan: Lots. In some countries, they beat you up and put you in prison
         if you go to church.

Julie: What a drag.

Jan: You know how many countries there are where you can't go
         to a supermarket and get all the groceries you need in one place?

Julie: Lots, I suppose.

Jan: Yep.

Julie: How come?

Jan: Because they have lots of little shops all over, and you have to
         go to a bunch of them to get everything you need.

Julie: Like they'd have a bubblegum shop one place, an ice cream
         shop somewhere else, and a meat store another place?

Jan: Something like that.

Julie: Yuk. I like it the way it is here. But I wonder what it would
         be like to live someplace that had bubblegum shops everywhere.

Jan: It would be sticky.

Julie: How come?

Jan: Because everyone would throw gum on the ground for people
         to step on.

Julie: Sounds like here.

Jan: Come on. Let's go watch the fireworks and be thankful we live
         in the good old USA.

(*Both exit.*)

July

The Vacation

Theme: Witnessing
Scripture: Romans 1:16
Characters: Stacy, Tom, Dad, Mom, Mr. Collins, Cecelia

Stacy: Guess what? I'm going on vacation.

Tom: You lucky duck. Where are you going?

Stacy: To the Gulf of Mexico.

Tom: Wow!

Stacy: I want to go, but I'm worried about my cat. She can't come with us, and I'm afraid she'll get lonely.

Tom: Who's feeding her?

Stacy: Our neighbor.

Tom: She'll be OK then. But if it will make you feel better, I'll come pet her every few days.

Stacy: That would be great.

Tom: Write me a postcard while you're there, and put a nice stamp on it for my stamp collection.

Stacy: OK.

Tom: And tell me all about your vacation when you get back.

Stacy: I will.

(*Both exit.*)

Dad: Isn't this scenery beautiful?

Mom: Yes. I love the mountains.

Stacy: Look at that deer!

Dad: Uh oh.

Mom: What's the matter?

Dad: I think we have a flat tire.

Mom: Oh, dear.

Dad: Here's a side road. I'll pull off on it.

Stacy: There's a fruit stand. Give me some money, and I'll buy a cantaloupe for us.

Dad: OK. It will taste good when I finish changing the tire.

Stacy: Give me one of those tracts, Mom. I'll give it to the people at the fruit stand.

Mom: What a nice idea. Here are two.

(*Stacy exits. Mr. Collins enters.*)

Mr. Collins: Having tire trouble?

Dad: Yes. But I have it just about changed, praise the Lord.

Mr. Collins: Isn't it awful to go on a vacation and have to put up with a flat tire?

Dad: Worse things could happen.

Mr. Collins: You're telling me! I just had to have a new head gasket put in my car.

Dad: That's a shame.

Mom: Last year on our vacation, our car gave up the ghost, and we had to buy a new one a thousand miles from home.

Mr. Collins: That's rough.

(*Stacy enters.*)

Stacy: Hi.

Mom: Stacy, this is Mr. Collins. He came to offer his help.

Stacy: Praise the Lord.

Mr. Collins: Your family sure uses that phrase a lot. I'll bet you didn't say that when you had to buy a new car last year.

Dad: As a matter of fact, we did.

Mr. Collins: You praise the Lord for problems?

Mom: Yes. In the Bible, we're told to praise the Lord for everything.

Mr. Collins: That beats anything I ever heard.

Stacy: Won't you stay and have a piece of cantaloupe with us, Mr. Collins?

Mr. Collins: I guess so. It sounds good in this hot weather.

Mom: I'll cut everyone a piece.

Dad: That canteloupe smells delicious. Let's give thanks for it before we eat. Stacy, would you like to?

Stacy: Dear God, thank you for this yummy fruit and thank you for Mr. Collins, who was nice enough to stop and offer to help us. In Jesus' name, Amen.

Mr. Collins: Er, that's the first time anybody's ever thanked God for me.

Dad: We'll keep praying for you too.

Mr. Collins: I can use all the prayers I can get. Now I'd better get back on the road.

Stacy: Bye. And remember, Jesus loves you.

(*Mr. Collins exits.*)

Dad: We'd better get back on the road too.

(*All three exit, then reenter.*)

Stacy: Look! There's the beach.

Mom: The water looks so inviting.

Dad: Let's go swimming.

Stacy: Whoopee, last one in is a baboon. (*She exits.*)

Dad: Let's walk in together. We'll be Mr. and Mrs. Baboon.

Mom: OK, Mr. Baboon.

(*Stacy enters.*)

Stacy: Look what I found.

Mom: What a pretty shell.

Dad: You're not wet yet!

Stacy: I didn't have time to get in the water. There were too many pretty shells to look at.

Dad: Let's go, Mom. Oh, that water feels good.

Mom: Stacy, I guess you're the baboon.

Stacy: Oops. I forgot about that.

(*Mom and Dad exit; Cecelia enters.*)

Cecelia: Your parents call you a baboon?

Stacy: It's a joke. I said last one in the water is a baboon. They beat me to the water.

Cecelia (*relieved*): Oh. What a funny custom.

Stacy: Are you from here?

Cecelia: Yes. My father runs the motel.

Stacy: What about your mother?

Cecelia: She left us.

Stacy: You mean she died?

Cecelia: No. She ran away with a rich American guest.

Stacy: Oh. That's too bad.

Cecelia: My father likes me to play on the beach. Then I stay out of his way.

Stacy: You can play with me a while. My parents will like to have you around.

Cecelia: They will?

Stacy: Sure.

Cecelia: You're very nice.

Stacy: I love you because God loves you.

Cecelia: You talk strange. First baboons. And now a God you say loves me.

Stacy: I'm a Christian. So are my parents.

Cecelia: Christians?

Stacy: Yeah.

Cecelia: You go to church on Sundays?

Stacy: And on Wednesday nights.

Cecelia: Ei, yi, yi. That's a lot of going to church.

Stacy: We like to because we get to worship and praise God with other people who feel the same way about God as we do.

Cecelia: Why do you like to praise Him?

Stacy: Because He loves us so much He sent His son Jesus to die so

our sins would be forgiven and we could be perfect in God's eyes
and talk with Him.

Cecelia: You mean God talks to you?

Stacy: Yes. And we talk to Him.

Cecelia: Ei, yi, yi. I would like to have a God like that.

Stacy: You already do.

Cecelia: I do?

Stacy: Yes. All you have to do is tell Jesus you will let Him come into
your life and that you accept Him as your Lord and Savior.

Cecelia: Then I can talk to God?

Stacy: It's that simple.

Cecelia: I will do it! Then when Papa doesn't want to talk to me,
I can talk to God.

Stacy: God will always listen.

Cecelia: Ei, yi, yi. This is so good. I'm very glad I met you.

(*Both exit. Stacy and Tom enter.*)

Tom: How was your vacation?

Stacy: Wonderful.

Tom: So is your cat. After I pet her, she followed me home. She's
been living at my house all week.

Stacy: She loves whoever pets her.

Tom: So tell me about your vacation.

Stacy: It was great. We passed out tracts at a fruit stand. We told
a man about how to praise the Lord for everything, and a little
girl I talked to accepted Jesus as her Savior.

Tom: But what about the ocean?

Stacy: We got to go swimming and found lots of pretty shells. But
the most fun thing was telling people about Jesus.

Tom: You sound like a little missionary.

Stacy: Nah. I'm going to be a business executive when I grow up.
But I'll always tell people about Jesus.

Tom: You're sure different.

Stacy: I should be. I'm a child of the King.

Tom: Royalty, huh?

Stacy: Yeah. I'm God's child, and I love to go around telling people
how neat He is.

Tom: I go to church too. But I don't talk to people about God like
you do.

Stacy: Try it some time. I'll bet you'll like it.

Tom: I'm going on vacation in two weeks. Maybe I'll try it then. If it backfires, no one I know will be around to see me make a fool of myself.

Stacy: Praise the Lord. At least you'll get some practice.

Tom: Will you take care of my goldfish while I'm gone?

Stacy: Only if they don't follow me home.

(*Both exit.*)

August

Bursting Barns

Theme: Giving
Scripture: 2 Corinthians 9:6-8
Characters: Don, James

Don: Twenty-five, fifty, one, two, two-fifty.

James: What are you counting?

Don: Money.

James: How much do you have?

Don: I'll tell you in a minute. Two-seventy-five, three, three-fifty. I have four dollars.

James: What will you do with it?

Don: Save it to buy a skateboard.

James: You'll have to save a lot more than that. Skateboards are expensive.

Don: I know. And I only get one dollar a week for allowance.

James: Me too. I've got six dollars, and I'm saving to buy a pair of cowboy boots.

Don: I wish we had a way to make money fast.

James: Maybe someone will hire us to do yardwork or something.

Don: I've already asked everyone in the neighborhood. They all said no.

James: Maybe we could get a paper route.

Don: There aren't any openings. I already checked.

James: Let's ask our dads for an allowance raise.

Don: Good luck. Mine said one dollar was more than he got when he was my age.

James: Then maybe we should try something really different, like tithing our money.

Don: Tithing on only one dollar? Are you crazy?

James: I'm serious. Mom and Dad say tithing is important. They're always reminding me about the widow in the Bible who tithed everything she had, even though it wasn't much.

Don: That's easy for your folks to say. They're rich. Tithing their money doesn't hurt because they have lots left over.

James: They're not rich.

Don: You have a new car every couple of years. You and your sister Sally always have new clothes, and you have a horse. That's better than most people I know.

James: Mom and Dad tithe 10 percent of what they make as their way of thanking God for what He gave them. They even give away money when God tells them to.

Don: God tells them to give away money?!

James: Sometimes.

Don: I wish God would tell someone to give me enough money to buy a skateboard.

James: If that's the way God wants you to get the skateboard, He'll tell someone to give you the money. But He usually doesn't work that way.

Don: Then how does He work?

James: According to my parents, first, you have to do everything you can to reach your goal. That includes tithing 10 percent of your money.

Don: But that would be 10 cents every week for me. Then I'd only have ninety cents left.

James: That's the way it is with me too.

Don: Have you tried tithing your allowance?

James: Sometimes. But it seems awfully expensive.

Don: I know what you mean.

James: We don't have much to lose by trying, though.

Don: If you'll tithe for one month, so will I. Then we can compare notes.

James: OK.

(*Both exit, then reenter.*)

Don: Hi, James. Where did you get those cowboy boots?

James: At a secondhand store.

Don: Did your parents buy them for you?

James: Partly. They were so impressed with the way I tithed my allowance that they pitched in the extra money I needed to buy the boots.

Don: Lucky duck!

James: I didn't feel so lucky every time the collection plate came around this month and I had to give up ten cents of my dollar.

Don: I know just how you felt.

James: Did you tithe your money too?

Don: No. I thought about it, but when offering time came, I kept thinking of all the things I could do with a dime. So I kept my money.

James: I'm going to have to tithe more than ten cents now.

Don: You've got to be kidding.

James: Nope. I got a job.

Don: You what?

James: I got a job helping Mr. Byrd clean out his garage and work around his place.

Don: You lucky stiff. Nobody had a job for me when I asked.

James: It's funny. Mom and Dad say that ever since I started tithing my allowance I've been getting more responsible.

Don: Big deal.

James: Well, it is sort of a big deal. I feel better about myself.

Don: I don't care about that. I just want to get a skateboard. And I sure won't get one by giving away ten cents of every dollar.

James: I figure God gave me that money in the first place, so the least I can do is give some of it back. Anyway, that's what the Bible tells us to do in Proverbs 3:9-10.

Don: What does it say?

James: It says to honor the Lord with your substance and with the firstfruits of your increase. Then you'll find your barns filled with plenty, and your presses will burst out with new wine.

Don: I don't want full barns and bursting presses. I want a skateboard.

James: I like the way tithing makes me feel sort of grownup.

Don: But look where it got you. If you'd saved all those dimes you put in the offering plate, you might have gotten a new pair of cowboy boots instead of a used pair.

James: I like these. You ought to try tithing. It might surprise you how good it makes you feel to thank God for what He's done by giving Him something. (*James exits.*)

Don: That guy is losing his marbles. If I give anyone something, I'll give James a piece of my mind for letting himself get brainwashed into giving money to God. God doesn't need his money. If I keep saving all my money, I'll have a skateboard by Christmas, and it won't be a used one. (*Don exits. Both boys reenter.*)

Don: Where did you get that skateboard?

James: I bought it with money I earned from Mr. Byrd.

Don: But I'm the one who wanted the skateboard.

James: I came by to give it to you.

Don: You're giving *me* this skateboard?

James: Yeah.

Don: Why?

James: Because you're my friend, and I want you to know I care about you.

Don: Boy, ever since you began your tithing experiment, you've been getting really weird. First, you give God money. Now you're giving me presents. You'd better start thinking of yourself.

James: I do. I want a train set. But it's very expensive, and I'm not going to get it unless I keep working very hard for Mr. Byrd.

Don: If you don't tithe the money he paid you, you'd get your train set faster.

James: God says He loves a cheerful giver, and I'm tithing my money cheerfully because I love God. He's been pretty good to me.

Don: You're weird.

Don: Maybe, but I've been pretty happy lately. It makes me feel good to give things to God and to you.

Don: I really like the skateboard, but I'm not sure I want to hang around with you any more. You're getting awfully goofy.

James: You ought to give tithing a try before you knock it so hard.

Don: Yeah? Well, maybe I will just to show you it doesn't work for everyone.

(*Both exit, then reenter.*)

James: A month has gone by, Don. Have you been tithing?

Don: Yeah.

James: Well, what do you think?

Don: Too soon to tell.

James: You can't fool me. I see that gleam in your eye. What happened?

Don: Well, I didn't get rich quick, that's for sure. But when Mom and Dad saw me tithing my allowance, they got to talking about it at home and decided to start tithing more too. It was the first time we'd talked about things like that as a family in a long time. It was kind of fun. Now we have a special time like that each week to talk about whatever we think is important.

James: That sounds neat.

Don: Yeah. They even listen to me. I told them what you said about being a cheerful giver.

James: Yeah?

Don: They thought it was pretty good. I heard them telling my neighbor, Mr. Holgate, about cheerful giving. They sort of bragged on me.

James: That's great.

Don: And you know what?

James: What?

Don: I was in the front yard playing catch with my dog when Mr. Holgate called me over to his yard. You know what he said?

James: No.

Don: He asked me if I'd weed his garden for ten dollars. I thought that was pretty funny.

James: What's so funny about that?

Don: Because I asked him two months ago if I could weed his garden. He said no because he always did it himself.

James: God gave you a blessing.

Don: Then my grandmother sent me five dollars.

James: It sounds like you've got bursting barns.

Don: Speaking of bursting barns, did you ever get that train set you wanted?

James: Funny thing about that. I saved up quite a bit of money, but I felt like I should give it all to Mrs. Barlow.

Don: Really?

James: It turned out she didn't have any money for food. When I gave her the money, she got this funny look on her face, like she was going to cry.

Don: I'm beginning to get it now. When we bless God by giving, that sort of opens a blessing door for other people. Like when our family got blessed by having special talks each week, and when you blessed Mrs. Barlow by giving her money.

James: I felt really good helping her. I don't know if I'll ever get my train set, but that doesn't seem so important any more.

Don: I guess you're not such a weird guy after all. I think I'll keep hanging around with you.

James: That's OK by me, pal.

(*They exit.*)

August

Last One to Miss Allen's House Is a Pig

Theme: Good Can Be Found Even in the Unpleasant
Scripture: Romans 8:28
Characters: Betsy, Mary, Mike

Betsy: I hate August.

Mary: How come?

Betsy: Because it's almost time to go back to school.

Mary: Ugh. Don't bring up that terrible subject.

Betsy: I hate school.

Mary: Me too. Except sometimes it's not so bad.

Betsy: Tell me one good thing about school.

Mary: Let's see. Uh, well, there's . . . recess.

Betsy: Even recess can be awful. Last year when we played jump rope, Cynthia decided she didn't like me. So she wouldn't let me jump.

Mary: You should have told the teacher.

Betsy: I did.

Mary: What did she do?

Betsy: Nothing.

Mary: If you can't look forward to recess, maybe you can look forward to lunch.

Betsy: Lunch is even worse. Those teachers on duty all tell you to eat faster and finish everything on your plate. Yuck!

Mary: You know what I like best about school?

Betsy: What?

Mary: Science.

Betsy: Yuck.

Mary: Last year in science we raised a guinea pig and learned how to feed it and take care of it. We even got to play with it.

Betsy: I remember hearing about that. Everyone called your room the pig sty.

Mary: How come? We kept it clean.

Betsy: Maybe so. But it smelled funny.

Mary: What about your room? You had bread mold growing all over the place.

Betsy: I forgot about that. Some of the mold turned green, yellow, and orange. It was fun to watch.

Mary: Library was fun, too.

Betsy: Yeah. Last year the librarian read us a story about this roly-poly bear who got stuck in a tight hole.

Mary: Winnie the Pooh!

Betsy: Yeah. That's him.

Mary: You know something else I like about school?

Betsy: What else is there to like?

Mary: Getting new clothes. Tomorrow Mom's going to take me shopping for some new dresses, slacks, and shoes.

Betsy: My mom's taking me next week when Dad gets paid.

(*Mike enters.*)

Mike: Hi, girls. What are you doing?

Betsy: Talking about school.

Mike: School!? How can you talk about such a horrible subject?

Mary: It's not so bad.

Mike: You mean you like all that spelling and math and stuff?

Betsy: Yuck. I hate spelling and math.

Mike: Then how come you're talking about school?

Betsy: Because, er, because . . . it's coming, and there's nothing we can do about it.

Mike: Maybe we can change all the calendars back one month.

Mary: Then we'd just have to go to school a month longer to make up for lost time.

Mike: Maybe we could blow up the school.

Betsy: Then they'd make us go to school in tents or churches or someplace else. Face it, Mike. School is coming. That's all there is to it.

Mike: I never give up. Maybe we could kidnap all the teachers.

Mary: They'd just hire new ones and throw us in jail.

Betsy: And send someone to jail to teach us. Yuck.

Mike: Maybe I should just run away.

Betsy: Someone would find you and make you go to school somewhere else.

Mike: Isn't there any way to get out of going to school?

Mary: Nope.

Mike: That's not fair.

Betsy: I know. But that's the way it is.

Mary: I'm looking forward to science, library, and getting new clothes, even though I don't like math.

Mike: New clothes. Who wants them?

Betsy: Mary and me.

Mike: You're just trying to impress the boys.

Betsy: Who'd want to impress boys? They don't care about clothes, anyway. All they care about is baseball and football and stuff like that.

Mike: Yeah! Last year Mr. Horton let us divide up in teams for sports during gym class. We played baseball, tag football, soccer, and volleyball. It was fun.

Mary: Why, Mike Sanders, I never thought I'd hear you admit school was fun.

Mike: I didn't say that.

Betsy: You did too.

Mike: Did not.

Mary: Did too.

Mike: I said sports was fun.

Mary: That's part of school.

Mike: I guess so, but it's only a small part.

Betsy: Remember last year when Mrs. Hermon's class cut up that frog?

Mike: Yeah. I heard Sarah fainted.

Mary: She did.

Mike: I wouldn't. I'd slice that sucker right up without blinking an eye.

Betsy: Maybe you'll get Mrs. Harmon this year.

Mike: I hope so. It's fun to be in her class.

Mary: You're slipping. You just said school was fun again.

Mike: I did?

Mary: Yep.

Mike: Well, maybe it's not *all* bad.

Betsy: I hope I don't get Mrs. Harmon. I don't want to cut up a frog.

Mike: Let's go find out what classes we're in.

Mary: How?

Mike: I saw Miss Allen's car in the schoolyard today. She ought to know since she's the school secretary.

Mary: OK.

Betsy: If I get Mrs. Harmon, I'll die.

Mike: Ah, Betsy, it's not that bad. She *could* make you *eat* the frog.

Betsy: Yuck. My stomach feels funny.

Mary: Don't pay any attention to Mike. If he had to eat a frog, I'll bet he'd turn green.

Mike: I'd turn into a monster and eat you with one big flick of my tongue.

Mary: You know what I'd do?

Mike: What?

Mary: I'd kiss that frog and make it turn into a handsome teacher.

Mike: You mean a handsome prince.

Mary: No. A handsome teacher. Then he'd march Mrs. Harmon
    into the hall and make her stand there for cutting up a poor,
    defenseless frog.
Mike: Silly. Let's find out who our teachers are. Last one to Miss
    Allen's house is a pig!
(*All exit, running.*)

September

The Brattiest Kid

Theme: Patience
Scripture: Luke 21:19
Characters: Hank, Freddie, Bill, George

Bill: Why are you sitting all by yourself?

Hank: I don't feel like playing ball.

Bill: I don't believe it. You looked forward to school all summer so you could play baseball at recess. Since school started, you've played ball every chance you get.

Hank: Not today.

Bill: What's wrong?

Hank: Oh, nothing.

Bill: Hey, this is me, Bill, your best friend. Remember? You can't fool me.

Hank: Oh, all right. That dumb umpire Mark and I got into a fight on the playground, and the rest of the kids wouldn't let me play any more. They called me a troublemaker.

Bill: Were you a troublemaker?

Hank: I'm never the troublemaker. It's always Mark. He hates me.

Bill: What happened?

Hank: I was up to bat, and the pitcher wasn't throwing right. So I ran over to tell him how to pitch better. Mark told me to stay at bat. I told him to lay off. We got into a fight, and the other kids chased me off the field.

Bill: Who was pitching?

Hank: Freddie.

Bill: You told *Freddie* how to pitch?

Hank (*pleased with himself*): Yeah.

Bill: Freddie's the best pitcher in the whole school.

Hank: He wasn't doing very well today.

Bill: What was he doing wrong?

Hank: Throwing lopsided.

Bill: What do you mean?

Hank: Just lopsided. Crooked. Weird.

Bill: Like in hard to hit?

Hank: Like in too far away to hit but not far enough away for the dumb umpire to realize it was a ball, not a strike.

Bill: How many strikes did you have before you told off the pitcher?

Hank: I didn't tell him off. I just tried to teach him a few tricks of the trade.

Bill: How many strikes?

Hank: Two.

Bill: How many balls?

Hank: None, because of that stupid umpire. I tried to explain the situation to him, but he wouldn't listen. So I thought I'd try teaching the pitcher how to throw better. But he didn't listen either. Nobody ever listens to me.

Bill: I do.

Hank: At least I have one friend. How come you're not playing baseball today?

Bill: I sprained my ankle yesterday. The doctor told me not to run or jump for a week.

Hank: Does it hurt?

Bill: I limp a lot, but if I'm careful, it doesn't hurt much.

Hank: I didn't notice you were limping. (*A bell rings.*) There's the bell. I'll race you back to class.

Bill: I can't run, remember?

Hank: Tough. You lose. (*Runs offstage.*)

(*Freddie enters and notices Bill limping to class.*)

Freddie: What's the matter, Bill?

Bill: I sprained my ankle yesterday. I have to walk kind of slowly.

Freddie: I wondered why you weren't playing baseball today.

Bill: The doctor says no baseball all week.

Freddie: You didn't miss much today. Hank pulled a temper tantrum. First he yelled at the umpire when he kept missing my new spin ball. Then he tried to tell me how to pitch. We finally chased him off the field. He left, calling everybody names.

Bill: Poor Hank. He doesn't know much about getting along with people. Maybe we can help him.

Freddie: I think he's beyond help. Nobody likes him.

Bill: If we show him we like him, maybe he'll improve.

Freddie: Sure. The sun will shine at midnight too. You know what he told me today? That I must have taken a bath in my mother's washing machine because my pitch was so wishy washy.

Bill: That's his idea of teaching you how to pitch.

Freddie: You're kidding. He can't even pitch a straight ball.

Bill: If we're going to help him, we've got to like him even when he's obnoxious.

Freddie: That's a tall order.

Bill: And not talk about him behind his back.

Freddie: How come? That's the fun part.

Bill: Because if we try to like him but say mean things about him at the same time, the two things cancel each other out. If we're going to like him, we've got to do it all the way.

Freddie: You mean like him for real?

Bill: For real. Let's pray for him.

Freddie: Whew! I'm only good at hating him, but I'm good at praying. Mom and Dad always ask me to say grace at breakfast. Dear Jesus, you know how bratty Hank is. Please do something to change him so he'll be fun to be around. Amen. Your turn.

Bill: Dear Jesus, you know what a hard time we have liking Hank. Help us to see him the way you see him, so we can love him like you do.

Freddie: We'd better hurry. We're already late for class.

(*Both exit. Enter Bill, Freddie, and Hank.*)

Freddie: How's the ankle, Bill?

Bill: It's been a week since I sprained it. The doctor says I can run on it if I'm careful.

Hank: That means you'll be slow. I hope you don't get picked to play on my baseball team.

Freddie: What a lousy thing to say to your friend!

Hank: Well, do you want him on your team?

Freddie: I'll take Bill over you any day.

Hank: That's because you're a fool. You can't pick a team any better than you can pitch.

Freddie: Why, you emptyheaded nobody!

Bill: Calm down, fellas.

Freddie: He just insulted you, after all you've done for him.

Bill: He's right. Whoever gets me won't have a fast runner. Maybe I can help the umpire by watching one of the base lines.

Freddie: You're too nice. You ought to kick him or something.

Hank: I'm leaving. You two are always arguing. (*He exits.*)

Freddie: The gall of that little monster. I prayed that God would change him, but He didn't. How can you be so nice to him?

Bill: I don't know. I just see Hank a little differently than I used to. I used to hate his guts. Now I see him hurting inside and being mean to people first so they can't hurt him first.

Freddie: That doesn't make sense.

Bill: Crazy, isn't it? But that's how he thinks.

Freddie: How do you get along with a jerk like that?

Bill: Love him no matter how mean he is.

Freddie: That's so incredible, you ought to make the front page of the newspaper. But I guess I'm willing to try liking Hank a week longer if you are.

Bill: It's a deal. (*They exit.*)

(*Enter Bill, Freddie, and Hank.*)

Freddie: You're running great now, Bill. Your ankle must be all well.

Bill: Yeah. It feels great. But you're limping. What did you do?

Freddie: I stepped on a nail.

Hank: That's too bad. Can you still play baseball?

Freddie: Yeah. But I can't run very fast.

Hank: That's OK. I hope you're on my team. You're a great pitcher. Hey, I see that new boy in school standing all by himself at the swings. I'll go over and say hello. (*He exits.*)

Freddie: I can't believe my ears. He actually said something nice to me.

Bill: Isn't it great?

Freddie: It's a miracle. Hank never says nice things to anybody.

Bill: Never say never.

(*Hank enters with George.*)

Hank: George, meet my friends, Freddie and Bill.

George: Hi. You dudes into anything besides baseball? I never saw a bunch of nuts as wild about baseball as you are in this weird school.

Hank: What do you mean, weird?

George: Just what I said. You're all a bunch of weirdos. Where I come from, they only play baseball in the spring.

Hank: It's not so bad once you get used to it.

George: It stinks. I wish I never came to this dumb school. (*He exits.*)

Hank: The nerve of that kid! I try to help him feel at home, and he bites off my head.

Freddie: Stick with us, Hank, and we'll give you lots of tips on how to get along with hard-to-get-along-with people.

Bill: Yeah. We've had lots of practice.

(*They exit.*)

September

The Leaf Paster

Theme: Fear of Change
Scripture: Isaiah 41:10
Characters: Jan, Sandy

Jan: You look all sticky. What have you been doing?

Sandy: Pasting leaves on our maple tree.

Jan: You've been what?

Sandy: Pasting leaves on the tree.

Jan: Why?

Sandy: Because they keep falling off.

Jan: They're supposed to fall off.

Sandy: Just because they fall every autumn doesn't mean they're supposed to.

Jan: Sure it does. The trees take a rest in the winter when it gets cold, and the leaves fall off. Then new ones grow in the spring.

Sandy: I think that's pretty dumb. I don't see why they can't just stay the same all year. Then we wouldn't have to rake leaves.

Jan: Is that what you're sore about? Raking leaves?

Sandy: I'm not sore. I'm just sticky. And I'm going to keep on being sticky until I get all the leaves in my front yard back on the maple tree.

Jan: That's ridiculous.

Sandy: I don't like it when things change so fast. One day the leaves are all green, then they start turning orange and yellow, and then before you know it they're falling all over the place. It just isn't fair.

Jan: The tree needs all its strength to get through the winter. It doesn't have time for frills like leaves.

Sandy: Well, I need its leaves.

Jan: How come?

Sandy: Because.

Jan: Because why?

Sandy: Because I . . . because I can't stand to see things change. It scares me not to know what's going to happen.

Jan: You're changing.

Sandy: I am not.

Jan: When was the last time you got a new pair of shoes?

Sandy: Two months ago.

Jan: Why did you get them?

Sandy: Because my feet got too big for my other shoes.

Jan: See? You *are* changing.

Sandy: Of course, silly. But I don't shed my leaves.

Jan: You shed your skin.

Sandy: Snakes do that. I don't.

The Leaf Paster

Jan: Sure you do. Every seven years your body has new skin.

Sandy: That's just normal wear and tear. I don't drop all that skin each year like a tree drops its leaves.

Jan: That's because you're not a tree.

Sandy: I *know* that, silly!

Jan: Then what's your problem?

Sandy: I don't have a problem. You asked me why my hands were sticky, and I told you.

Jan: I think pasting leaves on a maple tree is pretty dumb.

Sandy: And I think people who think pasting leaves on trees is dumb are dumb themselves.

Jan: I have an idea.

Sandy: What?

Jan: Why don't you gather all the leaves in one place and take them to the dump?

Sandy: Never! But maybe I can speed things up by spreading paste on all the leaves. Then I'll get Mom's hair dryer and blow them into the tree.

Jan: Oh, no!

Sandy: That's a good idea. I'll do it. (*Exits.*)

Jan: That's one mixed-up kid who doesn't realize that in autumn leaves are supposed to fall. The kid doesn't like anything to change, but life is full of changes, and Sandy is going to have to deal with that.

(*Sandy enters looking dejected.*)

Jan: What's wrong?

Sandy: I tried it. It didn't work.

Jan: What happened?

Sandy: When I put paste all over the leaves, they just stuck together. They were too heavy for the hair dryer to blow.

Jan: It's a good thing. If they had blown, they might have ended up on people's windows, roofs, cars, hedges, and all over the place.

Sandy: I guess so. And you know what else? I tried to put on the pasting smock I got for Christmas last year. But it wouldn't fit. I've outgrown it.

Jan: See? Just like the trees, you're changing.

Sandy: I really liked that smock. It had red and green polka dots.

Jan: Maybe your parents will give you a bigger one. Anyway, if you don't grow, how can you get as big as your folks?

Sandy: I could stand on a chair.

Jan: You'd look silly going through life standing on a chair.

Sandy: Maybe Mom can find me a smock as nice as the one I out-
grew.

Jan: Sure. That's what's neat about new things. You get to look
forward to them and wonder what they'll be like. It's kind of fun
to wonder what next year will be like. But we couldn't wonder
if everything stayed the same.

Sandy: I guess so, but I'm so stuck that autumn just isn't fun.

Jan: Why don't you quit trying to paste the leaves back on the trees,
let them worry about themselves, and just enjoy the changes
they're going through?

Sandy: Maybe I will. And I'll just let myself keep growing too and
enjoy all the new shoes and smocks I get.

Jan: Good idea.

Sandy: But someday I'll be big enough that I won't grow any more.
Then I'll keep all the same clothes forever.

Jan: Until they wear out or you get tired of them.

Sandy: Then what will I do? (*Sighs.*) I don't like change.

Jan: You can give the clothes to someone else. Like you can with
the leaves. How about if we find some pretty leaves you haven't
put paste on and take them to your teacher?

Sandy: Why?

Jan: Because, silly, they're pretty, and she'll like them.

Sandy: You really think so?

Jan: Cross my heart.

Sandy: OK. Why don't you help me put these pasty leaves in a
garbage bag for Dad to take to the dump. Then we'll have an
easier time finding leaves for our teachers.

Jan: That's the spirit.

(*They exit.*)

October

The Grouchy Neighbor

Theme: Loving the Hard to Love
Scripture: 1 Peter 3:9
Characters: Janet, Tony, Mom, Mr. Hopper

Janet: Complain, complain, complain. That's all Mr. Hopper ever does.

Tony: I know. Last night he made Dad get up at two in the morning to answer the door.

Janet: That wasn't Mr. Hopper. It was a policeman.

Tony: I know. But Mr. Hopper called the policeman.

Janet: It figures. He was probably complaining about barking dogs.

Tony: When the policeman shone a light in everyone's backyard, it wakened Frisky, and he started barking. So the officer knocked on our door.

Janet: That Mr. Hopper! If he complains one more time, I'll knock . . . knock his block off.

(*Dog barks.*)

Tony: Uh, oh. That sounds like Frisky. If she keeps on barking, we'll hear from Mr. Hopper again.

Janet: What's she barking about?

Tony: I don't know. (*Strains to look.*) Oh, I see. She's barking at a black cat.

Janet: Does that cat have a white tip on its tail?

Tony: Yeah. And it's eating food out of Frisky's dog dish.

Janet: That's Mr. Hopper's cat! *He's* making Frisky bark.

Tony: If Mr. Hopper complains now, we'll have a thing or two to tell him, won't we?

(*Mom enters.*)

Mom: Children, Mr. Hopper just called. He wants you to make Frisky stop barking.

Tony (*indignantly*): Frisky is barking at *his* cat.

Janet: And *his* cat is eating *Frisky's* dog food.

Mom: Now, children. Be kind. Mr. Hopper may have problems we don't know about.

Tony: He has problems *he* doesn't know about. His cat.

Janet: We should call him up every night and say, "It's 10 PM, do you know where your cat is?"

Tony: Hey, that's a neat idea. (*Both laugh.*)

Mom: Children, you'll do no such thing. Tony, shoo that cat away so he won't make Frisky bark.

Tony (*grudgingly*): OK. But I still think we ought to call Mr. Hopper tonight.

Janet: He's an old witchy goblin. If he goes trick or treating, he won't even have to wear a costume.

Tony: He's grown up. He doesn't go trick or treating.

(*Dog barks.*)

Mom: Tony, get rid of that cat.

(*All exit. Janet and Mom enter.*)

Janet: Mom, someone's knocking on the door.

Mom: Will you answer it for me, honey?

Janet: OK.

(*Mr. Hopper appears.*)

Janet: Oh. Mr. Hopper. Is our dog barking again?

Mr. Hopper: No, your dog is behaving itself. My wife just thought you might like to have this pie.

Janet: Mom, Mr. Hopper brought us a pie.

Mom: Hello, Mr. Hopper. Won't you come in?

Mr. Hopper: Thank you.

Mom: It smells like a cherry pie.

Mr. Hopper: It is. My wife loves to bake pies. But I can't eat them, and she can't eat a whole pie. So she makes a tiny one for herself and a larger pie for someone else.

Mom: That's very kind of her. If you could eat pie, I'd invite you to sit down and have a piece with us.

Mr. Hopper: Thanks. After I hurt my back, it did something to my digestion. Pies just don't settle well with me now.

Mom: Can you eat angel food cake?

Mr. Hopper: Yes.

Mom: Good. I just happen to have a couple of pieces. I'll wrap them up for you and your wife.

Mr. Hopper: Thank you.

Janet: How did you hurt your back, Mr. Hopper?

Mom: Now, Janet, that's none of your business.

Mr. Hopper: That's all right. I don't mind explaining. I used to work at building houses. I fell off a scaffolding and hurt my back.

Janet: You mean you fell all the way to the ground?

Mr. Hopper: I wasn't that high. Only two stories. But it was high enough to put me out of commission.

Janet: Is that why you always stay at home?

Mr. Hopper: Yes. I'm on disability.

Janet: You mean you can't work?

Mr. Hopper: No, I can't work. At least not in construction.

Mom: You must be in some pain then, Mr. Hopper.

Mr. Hopper: My back hurts all the time. I don't get much sleep any more. The slightest noise makes me jump.

Janet: That's too bad.

(*Tony enters.*)

Tony: I sure got rid of that cat. I plastered it with. . . . Oh. Uh, hi, Mr. Hopper.

Mom: This is my son, Tony.

Mr. Hopper: Hello, Tony.

Janet: His wife baked us a cherry pie.

Tony: Oh.

Mr. Hopper: I'd better be going.

Mom: Thank you for the pie, and don't forget your angel food cake.

(*Mr. Hopper exits.*)

Tony: A cherry pie won't make me forgive him for sending a policeman to our house in the middle of the night. And I fixed his cat! I threw wet mud balls at him. Now he's all covered with mud. I'll bet he'll think twice about coming back to this yard.

Janet: Mr. Hopper hurt his back.

Tony: I suppose he tripped over his own cat.

Janet: No. He fell off a spackeling.

Mom: That's a scaffolding.

Janet: Yeah. He fell off a scaffolding.

Tony: Too bad he didn't fall on his head.

Mom: Tony, that's not a nice thing to say.

Tony: It wasn't nice of him to send a policeman to our door at 2 AM either.

Janet: Mr. Hopper's back hurts so much he can't sleep very well. Every little sound wakes him up.

Tony: Then let him live in a soundproof house.

Mom: I don't think he can afford to, son. He's not able to work any more.

Tony: Oh. Well, I still think he's a mean man.

Janet: Now I feel sorry for saying such mean things about him. I don't think he's a witchy goblin any more. When I go trick or treating, I'll take him something nice for a present so he'll know I like him.

Tony: You're a soft touch. If he's going to make friends with the whole neighborhood, his wife is going to have to bake a lot of cherry pies, because everyone is mad at him for calling the police so often.

Janet: If we say nice things about Mr. Hopper, maybe they will start being nice to him too.

Tony: It won't work. Because he'll keep calling the police, and everyone will be mad at him all over again.

Janet: Then let's buy him a pair of ear plugs so he won't hear the dogs bark.

Tony: That's a good idea. Then he won't call the police.

Janet: We can give it to him when we go trick or treating. I have a dollar.

Tony: I have a dollar and fifty cents.

Janet: What if we don't have enough money?

Mom: You thought of such a good idea that I'll contribute whatever else you need. (*Mom exits.*)

Janet: Thanks, Mom. Let's go to the store, Tony.

Tony: OK. You know, I don't feel mad at Mr. Hopper any more.

Janet: Me neither. I don't think I'll call him up at 10 PM to ask him where his cat is.

Tony: But if that cat comes over again, I'll catch it, wrap it up, put it in a cardboard box, and mail it to Mr. Hopper!

Janet: You wouldn't!

Tony: No, I wouldn't, because I wouldn't have any money for postage. I'm spending it all on Mr. Hopper's ear plugs.

(*Both exit.*)

October

Gobbling Cookies, Watching Goblins

Theme: Jesus Conquered Satan
Scripture: Colossians 2:15
Characters: George, Henry

George: What's that?

Henry: My Halloween sack.

George: It sure looks scary.

Henry: That's to scare all the ghosts and goblins away.

George: But your sack has ghosts and goblins on it. How will they scare away other ghosts and goblins?

Henry: The ones on my sack are scarier than the ones I'll meet.

George: How do you know?

Henry: Because I got them out of the scariest book in the whole library.

George: Maybe there are scarier books in other libraries.

Henry: Are you trying to make me too scared to go trick or treating?

George: No. I'm just trying to tell you that you can't scare ghosts and goblins with other ghosts and goblins.

Henry: Then what can I scare them with?

George: You'll have to find something really powerful.

Henry: That's no problem. I'm going to be a big and powerful King Kong for Halloween. I have this really fierce mask. If that doesn't scare them away, nothing will. What are you going to be?

George (*sadly*): My parents say I can't go trick or treating.

Henry: That's awful. How come?

George: Because of all the razor blades and drugs and stuff some people put in treats.

Henry: I never got any treats like that.

George: Me neither. But my cousin Mark did. He found a razor blade in an apple and a pin prick in one of his candy bars. His mother made him throw away all his treats except for the things he couldn't eat.

Henry: Like what?

George: Like the ink pen he got and a little magnet to stick his artwork on the refrigerator.

Henry: I'll share my treats with you.

George: I hope you get some safe ones.

Henry: I will. All the bad things will have to stay away from me because my sack is so scary.

George: If that's true, how will anyone be brave enough to put treats in your sack?

Henry: I'll just knock on brave people's doors.

George: How will you know they're brave?

Henry: Because if they're really brave, they'll have a ferocious-looking jack-o'-lantern peering out their front window.

George: No one's afraid of a pumpkin.

Henry: They're not?

George: No. They're just like a big squash with places cut out to look like eyes, a nose, and a mouth.

Henry: Don't you think that's scary?

George: All it can do is sit where its owner puts it.

Henry: But it can sit there looking so fierce.

George: It only scares people who let themselves be scared.

Henry: *My* fierce designs on my sack are *genuine* goblin and ghost scarers.

George: No, they're not. If there really were ghosts and goblins, they'd be glad to see other things like themselves on your sack. They'd have to see something they are afraid of to scare them.

Henry: Like what?

George: Like you.

Henry: I'm not scary.

George: To things that are evil you are.

Henry: How come?

George: Because you've got Jesus living inside you. You scare them because Jesus came to destroy evil things.

Henry: Where does it say that?

George: In 1 John 3:8.

Henry: Wow! I need Jesus on my bag instead of ghosts and goblins.

George: No, you don't. You already have Jesus inside you.

Henry: But I never swallowed him.

George: Of course not. You just believe that He is the Son of God, and you accepted Him into your life and told Him He was in charge.

Henry: You mean all this time I've been worrying for nothing?

George: That's right. Because Jesus, who conquered all evil things, lives in you.

Henry: Then I can eat any treats I get!

George: Whoa! You have to use your eyes and common sense for that. My mom showed me how to check for bad stuff in candy. But she said sometimes it's hard to tell, and it's best to throw it all away unless someone you know real well made it.

Henry: But I want to go trick or treating. It won't be nearly so much fun if I have to worry about candy.

George: I've got an idea. Maybe we could just go to the houses of people we know real well.

Henry: The people I know real well are scattered all over town. Mom and Dad would have to drive all over the place, and they like to stay home on Halloween to see what costumes trick or treaters wear and to make sure no one plays tricks on them.

George: So do mine. I guess we'll just have to figure out something else to do on Halloween.

Henry: You know my favorite thing to do?

George: What?

Henry: I like to go to Aunt April's house and help her make chocolate chip cookies. Her cookies are so good you could eat a million of them.

George: Yum! I love chocolate chip cookies.

Henry: But she doesn't make them very often.

George: How come?

Henry: A lot of times she doesn't feel well, and it hurts her back to lean over the oven to put in and take out cookie sheets.

George: I know how to do that.

Henry: Me too.

George: That gives me an idea.

Henry: What?

George: For Halloween we can help Aunt April make cookies, so she'll have some for trick or treaters. Then she can give us cookies as a treat.

Henry: Yeah! Then we can take them home and eat them. (*Sighs.*) But it won't be as much fun as dressing up in my King Kong outfit.

George: You can still do that. Wear it on Halloween night. When trick or treaters come to the house, you can answer the door.

Henry: And beat on my chest and growl like King Kong and scare everybody.

George: And munch on Aunt April's cookies.

Henry: You can come over to my house in your costume and eat her cookies with me.

George: OK. We'll gobble cookies and watch all the goblins come to your door.

Henry: And we won't have to carry scary sacks to scare the goblins away, because we have Jesus in us.

George: This Halloween is going to be fun after all. I can hardly
          wait.

Henry: Let's go ask Aunt April if we can help her make cookies on
         Halloween and show her our costumes.

(*They exit.*)

November

Chief Heap Big Feast

Theme: Thanksgiving
Scripture: Psalm 107:22
Characters: Gary, James

Gary: Ugha, ugh, ugh. Mugga, mugga, ugh. Hooli gooli, mugga bugga.

James: Watch out, folks. Here comes Geronimo, the great warrior.

Gary: Me not Geronimo. Me . . . um, me, um, let's see, what was my name? Me Chief Heap Big Feast.

James: Never heard of him.

Gary: Miss Fillmore was right. The history books need-um to be rewritten.

James: Where should Chief Heap Big Feast appear in the new history books?

Gary: Right along with Governor William Bradford and Plymouth Rock.

James: You forgot to say um.

Gary: Plymouth Rock-um, sock-um.

James: You should have been a cheerleader.

Gary: Governor Bradford said-um that Dec. 13, 1621 should be-um set aside for feasting and prayer.

James: That's already in the history books.

Gary: But Chief Heap Big Feast isn't.

James: That's because he probably never existed.

Gary: You call-um me a liar?

James: Quit talking funny. Anway, Indians don't talk like that.

Gary: Chief Heap Big Feast talk-um any way he want-um to.

James: All right, all right. So who is he, anyway?

Gary: The pilgrims who came to Massachusetts long ago had-um heap bad weather the first winter. Nearly half of them died, squaws and all. But as bad as it was-um, the trip in boats from England was worse. Nobody wanted to go-um back. When summer and good weather came and they had nice crops of vegetables, they got-um happy. So Governor Bradford told them to set-um aside a day to give-um thanks because they were alive.

James: I know. But where do you come in, Chief Whatcha-ma-call-it?

Gary: Chief Heap Big Feast. My name demands-um respect or I scalp-um you.

James: Big deal.

Gary: Pilgrim women, they spend-um long days making feast. They boil, bake, roast-um food, enough for them and over eighty friendly Indians.

James: I suppose you're going to say you were there.

Gary: Of course. Chief Heap Big Feast bring-um his warriors, and they all bring-um wild turkey and deer meat for the feast. We all set-um outdoors like one big family to eat. There be-um prayers, sermons, praise songs for three days.

James: I'll bet you ate so much you popped your belly.

Gary: Chief Heap Big Feast never pop-um belly. He just pop-um jaw from chewing so hard.

James: You probably popped your jaw from talking too much in that silly Indian talk.

Gary: Don't make-um fun of the way I talk-um.

James: What I don't understand is if Governor Bradford declared Dec. 13 a day of Thanksgiving, why do we have Thanksgiving Day the last Thursday of November?

Gary: Because, oh boy of little knowledge, President Abraham Lincoln decided that's-um when it should be-um, and in 1941 the United States Congress finally decided-um he was right. They made-um Thanksgiving a legal holiday.

James: I can tell you've been reading your big brother's encyclopedias again.

Gary: If I'm going to be-um Chief Heap Big Feast, I have to know-um all about myself.

James: I've read about Thanksgiving in a lot of encyclopedias, and I never saw Chief Heap Big Feast mentioned.

Gary: Chief Heap Big Feast, he in big play written-um by my teacher, Miss Fillmore. She gave-um me the chief's part.

James: Oh, her. She's the one who wants to rewrite the history books.

Gary: That's-um her.

James: Who plays Governor Bradford?

Gary: Billy Morgan. He got-um the part because he is such a little squirt.

James: Was Governor Bradford little?

Gary: I don't know. Miss Fillmore just feels-um sorry for little people. So she gives them big parts.

James: She's short, isn't she?

Gary: Yeah. I didn't know you knew-um Miss Fillmore.

James: I don't. I just had a feeling she was short. You're not little. How did you get the part of the chief?

Gary: Because Miss Fillmore said-um I'm good at saying um. When she asks-um me a question in class, I always say, "Um, let's see, um, I know the answer. It's, um. . . . "

James: And you never quite get around to giving her the answer.

Gary: Somebody told you! Mom and Dad call-um me the heap big C and D kid. I get those grades because I don't answer questions.

James: Serves you right.

Gary: I'm on my way to practice-um for the play. I get-um to wear heap big bonnet of many feathers. They go-um all the way down my back.

James: Who plays President Lincoln?

Gary: Nobody.

James: Can I be President Lincoln?

Gary: He's not in the play.

James: Oh.

Gary: But you can be-um my water boy. He's not in the play either, but maybe Miss Fillmore will write him in.

James: What does he do?

Gary: It makes-um my throat dry to say all those ums. So you can follow me around with a glass of water.

James: That will be fun. You get too out of line with all those ums, and I'll dump the water all over your feathers. Then you'll be Chief Heap Big Wet Bonnet.

Gary: And you'd be in a heap of big trouble.

James: I'll be good. Take me to your teacher. I've never been in a Thanksgiving play before.

(*Both exit.*)

November

The Secret Weapon

Theme: Be Thankful for Everything
Scripture: Ephesians 5:20
Characters: Starla, Brad, Nancy

Starla: I hope the weather stays awful.

Brad: Why? It's snowing so hard we can't go outside and play.

Starla: I know. If it stays bad, our relatives can't come to our house for Thanksgiving.

Brad: I want it to be nice. If it doesn't get better fast, my family can't drive to Grandma's house for Thanksgiving.

Starla: We always stay home on Thanksgiving. Mom fixes a big dinner, and all our relatives come over.

Brad: Sometimes I wish I didn't have to go to Grandma's.

Starla: How come?

Brad: Because of my weird cousin Elmer.

Starla: What's wrong with Elmer?

Brad: He talks funny. He has these buck teeth, and when we laugh at him, he runs to his mother and tells on us. Then she goes to all the other adults, and they cuddle Elmer and give him treats. Then they bawl us out.

Starla: Sounds like Elmer spends a lot of time talking to the grown-ups.

Brad: Yeah. He's no fun to play with.

Starla: He doesn't sound half as bad as my cousin Freddie. He catches bugs. Then he chases the girls and puts the bugs down our backs.

Brad: My mom would roast me alive if I did that.

Starla: Last year he did it to me. That beetle felt awful climbing around on my back. I hope it keeps snowing so Freddie doesn't come this year.

Brad: If the snow keeps falling, I won't have to see Elmer.

Starla: Clouds, get darker. Snow, fall harder. Keep Freddie away on Thanksgiving Day.

Brad: Storm winds blow from the west and the east. Keep Elmer away from our Thanksgiving feast.

Starla: Do you think if we say it enough, it will happen?

Brad: Probably not. Nothing keeps Elmer away from food.

Starla: I think Freddie would walk through ten feet of snow to put bugs down girls' backs.

Brad: Face it. They'll never change. We're stuck with our weird relatives.

(*Nancy enters.*)

Nancy (*walks by without seeing Starla and Brad*):   Thank you for

Freddie. Thank you that he's going to behave himself on Thanksgiving. Thank you for Freddie. Thank. . . .

Starla: Nancy, what on earth are you doing?

Nancy (*startled*): Oh, Starla. Brad. I didn't see you.

Starla: Did you say, "Thank you for Freddie?"

Nancy: Yeah.

Starla: But he put a beetle down your back last year. Remember?

Nancy: How could I forget? I squashed it trying to get it off me. It made a big stain on my new yellow dress.

Starla: Then why on earth are you being thankful for Freddie?

Nancy: It's my secret weapon.

Starla: Secret weapon?!

Nancy: Yeah.

Brad: That beetle must have driven you crazy, Nancy. You belong in an insane asylum.

Nancy: Think what you want. But it works. (*Walks offstage saying, Thank you for Freddie.*)

Brad: She really *is* crazy.

Starla: Don't say things like that about my second cousin.

Brad: Well, have you heard anything so crazy?

Starla: No. Wait a minute. Yes, I have. I know where Nancy got that thank-you-for-Freddie stuff.

Brad: Wherever she got it, tell her to take it back!

Starla: She got it in Sunday School last week. Remember when the teacher said we were supposed to give thanks for everything because that's what the Bible says?

Brad: Yeah.

Starla: And remember Nancy asking if that meant you had to be thankful for horrible relatives?

Brad: Yeah. The teacher said it did. Then everyone booed.

Starla: That's right. And ever since, when I've been around Nancy, she's been mumbling to herself. I'll bet she's been thanking God for Freddie.

Brad: I'll thank God when Elmer goes home. Even better, I'll thank God if he gets sick and can't come.

Starla: Maybe you should thank God for Elmer and for what a nice person he's going to be this Thanksgiving.

Brad: Hogwash. Do you really believe it will work?

Starla: I don't know.

Brad: If I do that, you have to thank God for Freddie.

Starla: That's different. Elmer only has buck teeth. They stay in his mouth. Freddie has bugs. He puts them down people's backs.

Brad (*teasingly*): Does Freddie bug you?

Starla: Oh, hush.

Brad: Maybe Nancy has a good idea. I think I'll try it. Dear God, you said we're supposed to give thanks for everything. So thank you for Elmer. Thank you for Elmer. Thank you for Elmer.

Starla: I wouldn't be caught dead thanking God for Freddie.

Brad: Thank you for Elmer. Thank you for Elmer. That makes me remember something.

Starla: What?

Brad: Last year we played marbles. I lost my shooter and Elmer lent me his so I could win the game.

Starla: That was nice.

Brad: And he showed me how to make this extra neat paper plane.

Starla: Really?

Brad: He's awful when people tease him about his buck teeth. But I kind of hope he's there on Thanksgiving. I want to show him this neat book I found about how to make all sorts of paper designs. He's wild about things like that.

Starla: Freddie will never be interested in anything except bugging girls. He's a hopeless case.

Brad: Maybe you should be thankful for him anyway.

Starla: Never!

Brad: Then pretend and say, "Dear God, thank you for Freddie."

Starla: It won't work. I wouldn't mean a word of it.

Brad: Try it anyway.

Starla: Oh, all right. Just to make you quit bothering me. Dear God, thank you for Freddie and that he's going to behave decently at Thanksgiving. Thank you for Freddie. Oh, it's no use. Every time I think of him, I feel that awful beetle crawling up my back.

Brad: Keep saying it.

Starla: You mean about the beetle?

Brad: No. About being thankful for Freddie.

Starla: If you insist. Thank you for Freddie. Thank you for Freddie. Thank you for Freddie. (*Laughs.*) You know what Freddie did last year?

Brad: What?

Starla: He took the whipped cream off his pie and made a moustache and little beard on his face. Then he went around pretend-

ing to be Colonel Sanders. He walked up to Mom and said in this
funny deep voice, "What! No chicken today?" Even the adults
cracked up.

Brad: See? It's working.

Starla: What's working?

Brad: Thankfulness. You thought of something nice about Freddie.

Starla: I did, didn't I? He can be awfully funny. I guess I'd like him
if it weren't for the bugs.

Brad: Hey, look outside.

Starla: It stopped snowing!

Brad: And the clouds are breaking up.

Starla: Maybe it will be nice for Thanksgiving. I kind of hope it stays
nice.

Brad: Me too.

Starla: Weather, stay nice so Freddie can play
With Nancy and me on Thanksgiving Day.
But please chase all the beetles away.

Brad: Wind, don't blow, snow, don't fall,
So Elmer and I can have a ball
Making paper designs all over the hall.

(*Both exit.*)

December

The Almost Ruined Christmas

Theme: Giving in the Right Spirit
Scripture: 1 John 4:7-9
Characters: Carol, Heidi, Angie, Mother, Father, Patricia

Carol: Have you done all your Christmas shopping?

Heidi: I have gifts for everyone but Angie. I don't know what to get her.

Carol: She has everything. Her room is so full of toys she hardly has room to walk.

Heidi: I know. Most of them are mine. When Mom and Dad think I've outgrown them, they give the toys to Angie.

Carol: I'm glad I don't have any brothers or sisters. I would hate to give up Ollie.

Heidi: Who's Ollie?

Carol: My stuffed rabbit.

Heidi: I had a stuffed bear once. I called him Binky.

Carol: What happened to him?

Heidi: Mom and Dad figured I'd outgrown him, so they gave him to Angie.

Carol: That's enough to make a big kid cry.

Heidi: I wouldn't mind so much if she let me play with Binky. But she won't even let me come into her room.

Carol: Why?

Heidi: She's afraid I'll take my toys back. Fat chance. She breaks half of them before she's had them a week.

Carol: I don't think you want to give Angie a present.

Heidi: Yes, I do. I want to give her a punch in the face and a boot in the belly.

Carol: You do that, and you'll get a stick in the stocking.

Heidi: If I did that, I wouldn't get *any* stocking.

Carol: Give her a roll of garbage bags as a hint that she needs to clean her room.

Heidi: Perfect! Let's go the store right now.

(*Carol and Heidi exit. Angie and Patricia enter.*)

Patricia: What are you doing?

Angie: What does it look like?

Patricia: Wrapping presents?

Angie: That's right.

Patricia: But your whole room is full of presents.

Angie: That's because I'm getting rid of all my extra toys. Most of them used to belong to my older sister, Heidi. In fact, almost *all* my toys used to be hers. She's always trying to sneak into my room to steal them. So I'm giving them all away.

Patricia: Who will you give them to?

Angie: This lady down the street. She's a social worker. She knows lots of kids who don't get presents for Christmas. So she'll give them my toys.

Patricia: What are you wrapping now?

Angie: A bear. It used to be Heidi's. She called it Binky. That's such a silly name. I call it Bear. She's tried to steal this bear back more times than any other animal.

Patricia: Then why don't you give the bear to your sister for Christmas?

Angie: I've got a much better present for her.

Patricia: What?

Angie: That card over there.

Patricia: Is that all? Just a card?

Angie: Read it.

Patricia (*reads card slowly*): This card is to tell you that I have given away all your old toys to needy people. I know that will make you feel good, and you won't have to sneak into my room any more.

Angie: Isn't that a nice present?

Patricia: That's horrible. If you were my sister, I'd hate you.

Angie: No, you wouldn't. I wouldn't treat you like that because you wouldn't sneak into my room all the time.

Patricia: I think I'll go home.

(*Angie and Patricia exit. Carol and Heidi enter.*)

Heidi: That box of garbage bags looks like a really neat present when it's all wrapped and under the tree. Angie will never guess what it is in a million years.

Carol: Don't you think you should get her a nice present too?

Heidi: Her?! That bratty sister? She's not worth it.

Carol: What did she get you?

Heidi: I don't know. All I can find under the Christmas tree is a sealed envelope that says "To Heidi from Angie."

Carol: Tomorrow's Christmas. If you do decide to get Angie something nice, today's the last day you can buy it.

Heidi: My Christmas shopping is done.

(*Heidi and Carol exit. Enter Mother, Father, Heidi, and Angie.*)

Father: Merry Christmas.

Mother: Merry Christmas, everyone.

Heidi: When can we open our presents?

Angie: Let's do it now. OK?

Mother: You kids are always so excited about presents.

Father: Let's talk a little bit about Christmas first.

Heidi: Do we have to, Dad? We all know the story.

Angie: Yeah. We all know about Baby Jesus.

Heidi: And how the wise men and shepherds came to see the little baby born in a manger.

Father: But do you know why Jesus came?

Heidi: Of course. So He could grow up and become a man and teach people and die on the cross.

Angie: And come to life again.

Father: But why did He do all that?

Heidi: I don't know. His Father probably told Him to.

Angie: He did it because there were lots of prophecies that said He would do it, and if He didn't do what the prophecies said, they wouldn't come true.

Mother: You've got part of the picture, kids, but there's more.

Father: Jesus came because God loved people very much, but people didn't always love Him or each other. Sometimes they were very cruel to each other. Because they sinned, they couldn't walk and talk with God. It's like somebody who rolls in a mudhole and can't come inside a clean house until he washes up.

Mother: People were so dirty with sin they couldn't clean themselves up. The only one who could take away all the dirt was Jesus. The only way He could do that was to die and rise again. When He did that, He beat sin. Sin couldn't make people too dirty any more unless they let it. Now we can talk to God because we're clean from sin, thanks to Jesus.

Angie: But when we sin, we get all dirty again.

Father: Yes. But Jesus overcame that dirt. So all you have to do is ask Jesus to forgive you, and He'll take away the dirt. Then you can come into the clean house and talk to God.

Heidi: Good. Now let's open our presents.

Mother: All right. But don't both of you rush to the tree at the same time.

Father: I'll play Santa and hand each of you a present. Here's one for Mother.

Mother: It's a new bathrobe from all of you. Thank you!

Father: Here's one for Angie.

Angie: It's from Heidi. It feels big. Hey, you brat. Look, Mom and Dad. She gave me garbage bags.

Mother: Maybe she's trying to tell you to clean up your room.

Angie: But I already did. Give her that present from me, and she'll find out all about it.

Father: I think we're losing the Christmas spirit, girls. I hope you two don't start fighting again. Here's your present from Angie.

Heidi: An envelope. Is that all you gave me?

Angie: Open it.

Heidi: There's only a note in here.

Angie: Read it.

Heidi: It says, "This card is to tell you that I have given away all your old toys to needy people. I know that will make you feel good, and you won't have to sneak in my room any more." Mom, Dad, she even gave away Binky!

Mother: Binky?

Heidi: Remember my bear? The one you made me give to Angie?

Mother: Oh, yes. When you gave it away, it became Angie's to do with as she wished.

Heidi: But I didn't want to give it away. You made me.

Father: Oh, dear. Girls, you have turned Christmas into a day of hate. It's supposed to be a day of love. You've given each other spiteful presents.

Mother: What am I going to do with you? I've baked goodies all week to make Christmas enjoyable, and you girls have wrecked it. (*Begins to cry.*)

Father: Now look what you girls have done. You made Mother cry.

Heidi: I'm sorry. I didn't want to hurt you, Mom.

Angie: I'm sorry too. I don't feel very good about the present I gave you, Heidi. It wasn't a very nice thing to do.

Heidi: It was horrible. But I shouldn't have given you garbage bags.

Father: I think part of this may be our fault, Mother.

Mother: You're right. We've made Heidi give her toys away before she was ready to. And I don't think Angie likes getting lots of hand-me-down toys.

Heidi: Maybe we've all rolled around in the mud a little. Maybe we need to ask Jesus to clean us off.

Angie: Yeah. Then we can enjoy Christmas again.

Heidi: I can hardly wait to get you something nice for Christmas, Angie.

Angie: Me too. It's a lot more fun thinking of good things to give you than bad things.

Father: Let's start this day over again.

Mother: Let's do.

Father: Merry Christmas, everyone.

Mother: I think this time it really will be a Merry Christmas.

(*All exit.*)

December

I'm a Little Santa

Theme: Spoof on Santa
Characters: Puppets One and Two

Props: A piece of red material about two inches square with a piece
        of elastic attached to one end; a needle and thread

Puppet One (*sings to the tune of "I'm a Little Teapot"*): I'm a little
        Santa, short and stout.

        Here is my belly, here is my snout.

Puppet Two: Are you crazy?

One: No, I'm Santa.

Two: That song's supposed to be about a little teapot. How come
        you changed it?

One: Because, like I said, I'm Santa.

Two: You mean you're playing the part of Santa.

One: No, I'm Santa.

Two: You *are* crazy. There is no Santa. He just represents the spirit
        of giving and the spirit of love.

One: That's me. Giving and loving. Give me a present, and I'll love
        it.

Two: Are you ever mixed up!

One (*sings*): I'm a little Santa, short and stout.

        Here is my belly, here is my. . . .

Two (*interrupts him*): If you're so sure you're Santa, let's see you do
        something amazing.

One: Like sliding down a chimney?

Two: No.

One: Like making a toy?

Two: No. Santa's helpers do that.

One: But you said there was no Santa.

Two: There isn't.

One: Then how can he have helpers?

Two: What I mean is, in the stories we tell about Santa, his helpers
        make the toys.

One: Oh. Well, how about if I turn myself into a teapot? (*Sings.*) I'm
        a little tea. . . .

Two (*interrupts*): Cut that out! (*Thinks.*) I know! If you really think
        you're Santa, turn one of those kids out there into a reindeer.

One: What kids?

Two: Those kids.

One (*looks*): Oh, *those* kids.

Two: If you can do that, then maybe, just maybe I'll believe you're
        Santa.

One: A reindeer, huh? What if they don't want to be turned into a reindeer?

Two: Why don't you ask them?

One: Ask them? (*Gulps.*) Uh, OK. Hey, kids, any of you want to be changed into a reindeer? (*Quickly turns his back.*)

Two: How are you going to tell if there are any volunteers if you don't look?

One: Uh, I thought someone might be behind me.

Two: Well, you better ask for volunteers again.

One: Well, OK. Who wants to be changed into a reindeer?

Two: Anyone want to volunteer? (*A preselected adult from the audience should announce whether there are any volunteers and should pick which child should be chosen if there is more than one volunteer.*)

IF THERE ARE VOLUNTEERS, CONTINUE BELOW. IF NO VOLUNTEERS, GO TO THE HEADING "IF THERE ARE NO VOLUNTEERS."

Two: Okay, kid. Come up here. (*Have the child come behind stage.*) Now, let's see you change that kid into a reindeer.

One: All right. But you stay here while I'm gone.

Two: OK, but hurry.

(*One exits. While backstage, he takes the red material with the elastic, fits it to the child's head, and sews the loose end of the elastic to the end of the material that doesn't have elastic attached to it. Then he fits the material over the child's nose with the elastic securing it behind the child's head. Then he sends the child back into the audience. Two ad-libs about One being crazy and how there is no way to turn a child into a reindeer.*)

One (*enters*):   Well, what do you think?

Two: Think about what?

One: About my reindeer.

Two: What reindeer?

One: That reindeer!

Two: That's not a reindeer. That's a kid with a piece of red material on (his) (her) nose.

One: Rudolph has a red nose. So that's Rudolph, the red-nosed reindeer.

Two: All right. Let's see him fly.

One: Fly? (*Go to heading "Conclusion."*)

IF THERE ARE NO VOLUNTEERS

Two: No volunteers. Well, you'll just have to admit you're not Santa.

One: Wait a minute. I could change *you* into a reindeer.

Two: Me?!

One: Why not? If I'm really Santa, I can change anyone into a reindeer.

Two: Oh, well. What harm would there be? You can't do it, anyway.

One: OK. I want you to go to bed. When you get up, you'll be a reindeer.

Two: All right, but you know it won't work. (*Exits. While he is offstage, the red piece of material with elastic should be fitted around Two's nose, held securely to his head by the piece of elastic.*)

One (*while Two is offstage getting the material fitted to his nose, One sings*): I'm a little Santa, short and stout. Here is my belly, here is my snout. (*He continues singing until Two is ready to come back onstage.*)

(*Two enters with the red material on his nose.*)

One: Hi, Rudolph. Will you agree now that I'm Santa?

Two: My name's not Rudolph.

One: Sure it is. I changed you into a reindeer, and because you have a red nose, I know you're Rudolph, the red-nosed reindeer.

Two: Hmph. You haven't changed me. You just made me have a red nose.

One: You look like Rudolph to me.

Two: All right. Let's see you make me fly.

One: Fly?

(*Go to heading "Conclusion."*)

CONCLUSION

Two: Yeah. Rudolph flies, according to the make-believe stories.

One: I can tell that nothing will convince you I'm Santa.

Two: I will be convinced if I see *you* fly.

One (*thinks*): OK. I'll fly.

Two: This I've got to see.

(*One moves all over stage pretending to fly.*)

Two: You're not really flying.

One: If I'm not flying, then what am I doing?

Two: Making a fool of yourself.

One: I'm no fool. I'll show you. I'll get on my sleigh with my eight trusty reindeer and fly all over this room.

Two: Impossible.

One: How come?

Two: Because you're not Santa.

One: If I'm not Santa, then who am I?

Two: Beats me. I never saw you before.

One: I know who I am. (*Sings.*) I'm a little teapot, short and stout. Here is my handle, here is my spout.

Two: I can't bear to go through this again. OK, you're a little teapot. And I'm leaving. (*Exits.*)

One: Whew! He's gone. Now I can start delivering my presents. Merry Christmas, everyone! (*From behind stage, candy is thrown into audience. One exits, singing.*) I'm a little Santa, short and stout. Here is my belly, here is my snout.

December

Mystery of the Cave

Theme: The Christmas Story
Scripture: Luke 2:6-7
Characters: Eliakim, Zadok, Obed

Eliakim: Zadok, can you come out and play?

Zadok (enters): Hi, Eliakim. Did anyone see you? You know what our fathers said they'd do if they caught us together again. They think we get into too much trouble.

Eliakim: No one saw me. How about you?

Zadok: No. Mother was too busy bawling out Judith for getting sand in the flour, and Father was sharpening his garden hoe. I was supposed to help him, but after I broke his good sharpening stone, he told me to get lost.

Eliakim: My parents were so busy arguing about what to serve at my big sister's wedding that they didn't see me sneak out. Look, I even took my special walking stick, the one I'm only supposed to use on very special occasions.

Zadok: Your parents will be mad if they catch you.

Eliakim: They won't catch me. Watch this. I'm a member of the Sanhedrin walking to Jerusalem to decide an important case.

Zadok: What case, silly?

Eliakim: The case of what will happen to Eliakim for using his walking stick on an unimportant occasion.

Zadok: I'm a member of the Sanhedrin too, and I declare you shall stand on your head while your sister runs around you ten times in her wedding dress, dumping perfume on you every time she passes your feet.

Eliakim: Throw this man out of the Sanhedrin for being mean to his fellow council member.

Zadok: Hey, look! Widow Dorcas's chickens! Let's open the gate and let them out.

Eliakim: OK! Remember how she screamed and ran around with her broom the last time we did that?

Zadok: It was so funny, I almost died laughing.

Eliakim: Help me open the gate.

Zadok: There they go! Look at their feathers fly.

Eliakim: Uh, oh. Let's get out of here. Here comes Widow Dorcas with her big son Jotham. He'll skin us alive if he sees us here. (Both boys run across stage.)

Zadok: We can hide in Obed's cave. Jotham won't think to look for us here.

Obed (enters): Boys, stay out of that cave. I have guests in there tonight.

Eliakim: Guests? In your cave? What's wrong with your inn?

Zadok: Yeah, what's wrong? Too many bedbugs?

Obed: Dear God in heaven! I know both your fathers. Neither deserves such sons as you.

Eliakim: I don't believe you have guests in there. You're hiding something.

Obed: What is the world coming to? With boys like you, this country has no hope. Haven't you heard of Caesar Augustus' decree that everyone must register in his own city to be taxed? You'd think the whole country came from Bethlehem the way they flock here. The inn's full. Now the cave's full, and people keep coming. Where am I going to put them all?

Zadok: On a slow donkey cart to Jerusalem.

Obed: Ei, yei, yei! Advice like that will get me thrown in jail by the Roman soldiers. The Romans want their tax money, and I must cooperate.

(*Both boys whisper to each other, then make a dash toward the cave.*)

Obed: Leave my guests alone, you hear? Or I'll tell your fathers about your terrible behavior. Now go! (*He herds them offstage. Eliakim and Zadok reenter.*)

Eliakim: Do you believe Obed really has guests in there?

Zadok: Of course not. Something's going on in there he doesn't want anyone to know about.

Eliakim: Like what?

Zadok: I don't know. Maybe he's a thief, and he's storing stolen property there.

Eliakim: No. The cows and donkeys would get it all dirty.

Zadok: Well, maybe he's hiding people in there so they won't have to register to pay their taxes.

Eliakim: He's too scared of the Roman soldiers for that.

Zadok: Then what *is* going on in that cave?

Eliakim: I don't know. Look, someone's coming. Squat down behind this bush.

Zadok: Nothing to worry about. They're just shepherds. They won't hurt anyone.

Eliakim: They're going into the cave!

Zadok: This is crazy! What are shepherds doing in there?

Eliakim: I don't know, but it looks very strange.

Zadok: Now they're coming out. Look at their faces.

Eliakim: I've never seen shepherds look so happy before. What do they have to be happy about?

Zadok: Somebody inside that cave must have given them something.

Eliakim: Like what?

Zadok: I don't know. Maybe a thousand shekels or something.

Eliakim: A thousand shekels would make me smile too. Then I'd buy seven walking sticks, one for each day of the week.

Zadok: Oh, oh. Duck down. Here come some more people.

Eliakim: They're weird looking. They couldn't have come here to register for the Roman tax. They're foreigners. Look at their long, fancy clothes and funny hats.

Zadok: And look what they're carrying!

Eliakim: Gold!

Zadok: One guy has myrrh.

Eliakim: And the third has frankincense. I can smell it.

Zadok: They've got to be rich.

Eliakim: Then how come they're hanging around a cave with some shepherds?

Zadok: There's more to this than meets the eye. I'll bet we have some illegal activity on our hands.

Eliakim: You mean like crime?

Zadok: I mean like . . . I've got it. Gambling! They're gambling in there, Eliakim. The shepherds won something nice, and now the strange men are trying their luck.

Eliakim: They're leaving without their gold and stuff. They must have lost. We'd better report this to the town council.

Zadok: No. Let's hang around. Maybe we can sneak in and do some gambling ourselves.

Eliakim: Are you crazy? If we get caught, they might cut off one of our fingers. That's what they did to Jonathan for stealing apples from the merchants.

Zadok: We'll be real sneaky. No one will see us, and whoever is in there won't tell on us. That's for sure.

(*Obed enters.*)

Eliakim: Get down! Here comes Obed.

Obed: I saw you!

Zadok: Rats! The sky is so bright tonight, we can't hide from anyone.

Obed: Get out of here, boys. I won't have my guests disturbed. Now scram! (*Both boys exit.*) Rooms to clean. Guests to keep happy.

Meals to fix. And these pesky boys. Will this busy time never end? (*He exits.*)

(*Zadok sneaks back onstage.*)

Zadok: Come, Eliakim. He's gone.

(*Eliakim enters.*)

Zadok: Yo go into the cave first.

Eliakim: Me?! It was your idea.

Zadok: You're four months older. You go first.

Eliakim: All right. But you stay outside to warn me if anyone comes. I'll take my walking stick with me just in case.

Zadok: Don't be scared.

Eliakim: Don't be scared, he says. I'm the one who could lose a finger. (*He exits.*)

Zadok: I wish he'd hurry up. It can't take that long to see what's going on in there.

(*Eliakim comes onstage without his walking stick, looking dazed. Walks past Zadok without seeing him.*)

Zadok: Eliakim!

Eliakim: You'll never believe what's in there, Zadok.

Zadok: So tell me.

Eliakim: Go look for yourself.

Zadok: You left your walking stick in there.

Eliakim: I gave it away.

Zadok: You mean you gambled and lost it. No wonder it took you so long. Your parents will beat you for losing it.

Eliakim: I didn't lose it. I wanted to give it away.

Zadok: What did they do to you in there? Make you drink strong wine?

Eliakim: Go see for yourself.

Zadok: OK, OK. (*Exits.*)

Eliakim: Widow Dorcas's chickens are out. I'll help her catch them. Here, chicky. Here, chicky.

Zadok (*enters, looking dazed*):   I've never seen anything like it.

Eliakim: Obed really did have guests.

Zadok: Yeah. Wasn't that baby something?

Eliakim: Yeah. That mother was something too.

Zadok: And the father. Did they talk to you?

Eliakim: Yes. She said the shepherds and strange men came to visit because the baby is a king.

Zadok: That's what she told me too.

Eliakim: Did the baby look at you?

Zadok: Yeah, and he gooed and slobbered.

Eliakim: He didn't look like a king.

Zadok: But it felt like a royal place in there.

Eliakim: Yeah, like someplace real special, real peaceful and nice.

Zadok: What were you doing just now?

Eliakim: Helping Widow Dorcas round up her chickens.

Zadok: Need some help?

Eliakim: No. I think I got them all.

Obed (*enters*): You again? Get out, both of you.

Zadok: Don't be upset, Obed. We won't bother your guests.

Obed: Oh, now you believe I have guests. What made you change your minds?

Zadok: We saw the baby.

Eliakim: And his parents.

Obed: You disturbed my guests! I knew I should have told your parents about your wicked behavior.

Zadok: They were nice to us. And, besides, we weren't the only ones to visit them. Shepherds and foreign men dressed real funny visited them too.

Obed: Ei, yei, yei! So many intrusions. Now my guests will never return to Bethlehem, and they'll spread the word about how terrible my inn is. My business will be ruined.

Zadok: No, it won't. Your guests liked all their visitors.

Eliakim: Yeah, and they said their baby was a king.

Obed: There you have it. What parent isn't proud of his child? But a king. That's going a bit too far.

Zadok: Can we help you clean up the inn, Obed? You must be tired with all your visitors.

Eliakim: We're good at sweeping.

Obed: Help me? Sweep? What's come over you boys? You were never nice like this before.

Zadok: It's your cave guests.

Eliakim: They're very special.

Obed: If I'd known guests in my cave would cause such miracles, I would have put people out there long ago. Before you start to help me, we must talk about your work. I never let people work without pay. A merchant stayed at the inn a few weeks ago and left two fancy walking sticks. I have no use for them. You may each have one for helping me.

Zadok: Wow.

Eliakim: I gave the baby one stick, and we're getting back two! He really must be a king.

Obed: What?

Eliakim: Oh, nothing.

Obed: Come on. I'll put you to work cleaning rooms while you're still in a helpful mood. (*Both boys exit.*) Boys! I never will figure them out. Mean one minute, nice the next. Maybe there's hope for us after all. (*He exits.*)

492- 9902